A B C D E F G

Z

Y

X

W

V

U

ALPHABETS &
-·SAMPLERS·-

T S R Q P O

H

I

J

K

L

M

N

ALPHABETS &
·SAMPLERS·

40 Cross Stitch and Charted Designs

Brenda Keyes

Tho our Countrie everywhere is fil'd
With ladies and with gentlewomen skil'd
In this rare art, yet here they may discerne
Some things to teach them if they list to learne
And as this book some cunning workes doth teach
Too high for meane capacities to reache
So for weake learners other workes here be
As plaine and easie as an ABC

THE NEEDLE'S EXCELLENCY.
PUBLISHED 1631

David & Charles

FOR CHRIS

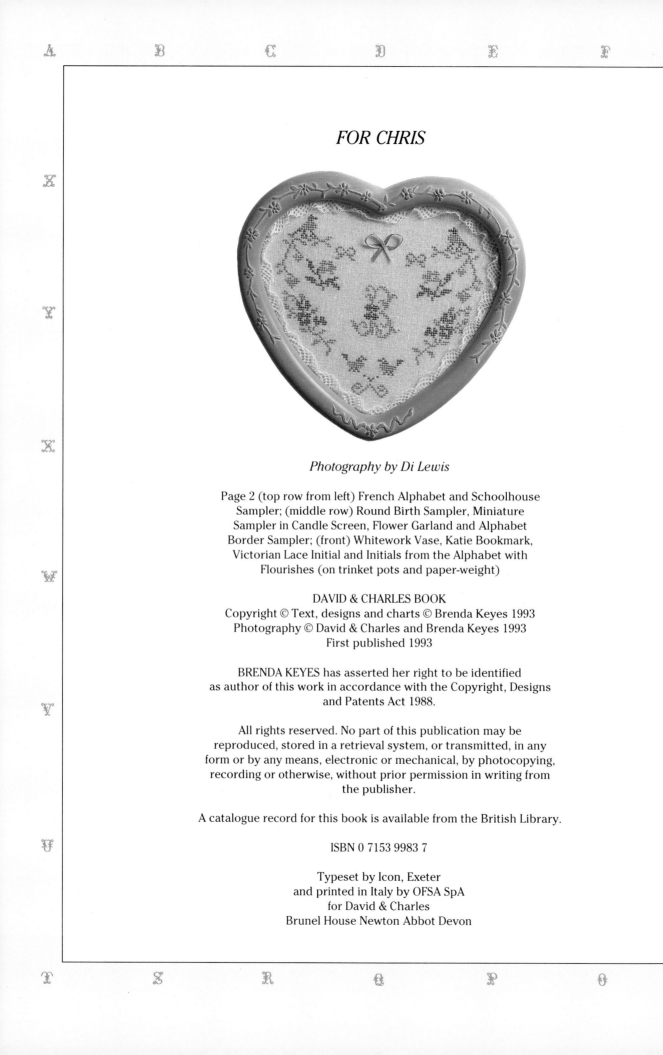

Photography by Di Lewis

Page 2 (top row from left) French Alphabet and Schoolhouse
Sampler; (middle row) Round Birth Sampler, Miniature
Sampler in Candle Screen, Flower Garland and Alphabet
Border Sampler; (front) Whitework Vase, Katie Bookmark,
Victorian Lace Initial and Initials from the Alphabet with
Flourishes (on trinket pots and paper-weight)

DAVID & CHARLES BOOK
Copyright © Text, designs and charts © Brenda Keyes 1993
Photography © David & Charles and Brenda Keyes 1993
First published 1993

BRENDA KEYES has asserted her right to be identified
as author of this work in accordance with the Copyright, Designs
and Patents Act 1988.

A catalogue record for this book is available from the British Library.

ISBN 0 7153 9983 7

Typeset by Icon, Exeter
and printed in Italy by OFSA SpA
for David & Charles
Brunel House Newton Abbot Devon

CONTENTS

INTRODUCTION

Alphabets have always been a source of fascination for me, and especially so when used in embroidery. Alphabets and numerals began to appear regularly on samplers from the beginning of the eighteenth century. This was largely due to the fact that the purpose of working a sampler had changed from one of creating an embroidered record of interesting designs to that of training the worker for the task of marking household linen. Practically all samplers were worked in schools and many bore a religious or pious text. Not all, it must be said, were worked out of a love of embroidery. My favourite verse reads 'Alice Parker did this writ and hated every stitch of it'.

Happily, this sort of enforced and resented needlework is a thing of the past. Samplers are still sewn today, either in admiration and imitation of those worked many years ago, or as modern versions of the craft to commemorate special occasions – Birth and Wedding Samplers, for example. Whatever the reason, it is fascinating to think that the samplers we sew today will most probably provoke as much interest in years to come as those earlier pieces we so admire.

The aims of this book are two-fold, firstly to provide the embroiderer with a comprehensive range of charts and patterns for initials, alphabets and samplers, and secondly to encourage adaptation of these or, indeed, any other charted designs. Where appropriate, alternative ways of completing the design have been suggested, but it must be stressed that these suggested alternatives are but a drop in the ocean compared to the myriad design possibilities. My hope is that, eventually, after the embroiderer has mastered the basic techniques, she or he will view any of the designs given as simply one possibility for that particular project and then go on to adapt themes and ultimately create original designs.

Traditional Alphabet Initial
with Border, and the
Schoolhouse Sampler

WORKBOX

All the designs in this book are 'counted' needlework. This simply means that they are worked from a chart as opposed to being printed on the fabric or canvas. Once you have mastered this technique of 'reading' and then 'translating' the chart to fabric, you will not look back. This method opens up so many design possibilities. It will not only enable you to alter, enlarge or reduce any charted designs you may have but also, with practice, will enable you to create your own designs quickly and easily.

How to 'Read' a Chart

Charts can be in black and white or colour. They may consist of coloured squares, symbols, or coloured squares with symbols. Each symbol or coloured square represents a different thread colour. The method for 'translating' them, however, remains the same. One square on the chart containing a symbol or colour represents one stitch (usually cross stitch) on your fabric. The blank squares represent the unworked fabric. Straight black lines, often surrounding a motif, indicate back stitch. The key will indicate the colours to use.

Threads

Such a wonderful variety of threads is available today that the design possibilities are endless. What would the dedicated and skilled needleworkers of the past have made out of what is now available? It is quite humbling to think of the incredibly detailed masterpieces that were created out of the limited resources of the day. Luckily for us, no such problem now exists and the only limit to excitingly colourful work is our own imagination.

The most commonly used thread for cross stitch is stranded cotton (floss). This thread is treated by a process known as mercerisation to give it a polished sheen like silk. The range of colours is enormous and it is widely available. The number of strands used depends on which fabric you are working and also on the effect you wish to achieve. Generally speaking, most counted cross stitch designs are worked with two strands of stranded cotton over one block of Aida or two threads of linen. Outlines are usually worked with one strand (or two for more definition).

Flower threads – Danish, German and French – have a matt finish, are single ply and very versatile. Try working part of your design in flower thread and part in stranded cotton. The contrast between the matt and polished threads will greatly enhance your work.

Although these two threads are the most commonly used for counted thread needlework, there is no reason at all to limit yourself to them. Experiment with some you might not have tried before – perlé cotton, soft cotton, silk, gold and silver threads, metallic thread, fine wool, Marlitt, space-dyed threads, the list is endless. The substitution or addition of some of these threads can make a somewhat ordinary piece unique and far more visually appealing.

Thread Storage

There are many types of thread organiser on the market today, among them cards with punched holes to hold cut skeins, storage boxes with cards to wrap thread around and plastic pages with pockets to hold entire skeins. Whichever method you choose (including your own versions of the above), storing your threads in an organised and efficient manner makes sense. As well as keeping your threads clean and tangle free, it will enable you to see at a glance the colours available and therefore save you time when choosing them.

Needles

Blunt tapestry needles are needed for counted needlework. The size depends on the fabric and thread you intend to use. The needle should be able to pass through the fabric with only slight pressure. Try to keep in stock at least one packet each of sizes 20, 24 and 26 (the most commonly used) as not only does it make life a lot easier to use the correct needle but, as you will quickly come to realise, you will lose at least every other needle you own!

Fabric

The popularity of charted designs for counted needlework has prompted a huge increase in the fabrics now available for this type of work. The most important qualification for a fabric suitable for counted needlework is that it must have an evenweave, ie the same number of threads horizontally and vertically. Aida and Hardanger fabrics are a popular choice as they are woven from cotton to produce clearly defined blocks of fabric which are particularly easy to count and work on. Aida fabric is available in many colours and 'counts' or number of blocks per inch (25mm). The most commonly used are 14 count and 18 count. Other evenweave fabrics to try are Lugana, Davosa, Jubilee and Floba. Check which fabrics and colours are available at your local needlework shop before deciding what to work on. You may be surprised and delighted at what they now have to offer and a relatively simple piece can be transformed by working on a more exciting fabric.

Linen

Most of the wonderful samplers I have admired from the past have been worked on linen and I see it as being essential for heirloom quality pieces. Linen is not difficult to work on. It simply means counting two threads to work over instead of one block. (This is usually the case but some very fine work requires you to work over just one thread. This could cause problems if your eyesight is less than perfect, but in most cases, if you work in a good light and/or with the addition of a magnifier, working over one thread is only slightly more difficult than, say, working on 18-count Aida.) The advantage of working on linen as opposed to 'block' fabrics, apart from the wonderful appearance and feel of the fabric, is that it is possible to work part of the design over two threads and part over just one. This is a definite advantage when working certain samplers where the verse, for example, is worked over one thread and the rest of the design over two. It gives a more balanced feel to the design if the verse does not take up the majority of the space. If you study antique samplers you will see many examples of this method of working.

Hoops and Frames

An embroidery hoop can be a very useful aid to accurate stitching. Whenever possible, use a hoop that is big enough to house a complete design comfortably. This will ensure that the hoop does not need to be placed over the stitching and will thus avoid pulling and snagging completed work. Hoops also tend to leave creases that are almost impossible to remove even if you remember to take the hoop off every time you finish stitching. One way to prevent your fabric slipping about is to bind the inner hoop with white bias binding secured with a few stitches. You may also like to protect your work by placing tissue paper between fabric and hoop and tearing away the middle section, leaving the section to be worked exposed.

Rectangular frames are more suitable for larger pieces of work and they come in many sizes, including large free-standing floor frames. The side edges of the fabric are hemmed or bound with tape to strengthen them, and then the top and bottom edges of the fabric are sewn to the webbing which is attached to the top and bottom rollers of the frame using strong thread. Care must be taken to ensure that the fabric is evenly placed in the frame as if sewn in unevenly it will

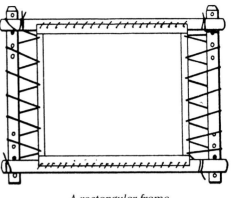

A rectangular frame

become distorted. The frame is then assembled and the side edges laced to the stretchers with very strong thread (see Figure).

A quicker and easier method than this is to buy a selection of ready-made rectangular frames, available from some embroidery shops, or make your own from stretcher bars – on sale in art shops. (If possible buy the ready-made variety as they are lighter.)

The fabric is then stapled straight onto the frame (or attached with drawing pins) saving a great deal of time and effort. Although these frames do not look as elegant as roller frames, they serve their purpose well, providing you use a large enough frame to allow sufficient fabric for lacing and finishing. Also, they have no protruding corners which might catch your thread, they are easier to store, and more portable.

Cutting your Fabric

Always allow ample fabric around the design area, at least 4–6in (100–150mm), although smaller pieces – miniatures, brooches etc – will not require this much excess. Measure carefully and always cut along a thread line using dressmaking scissors. If you intend to substitute a fabric for the one suggested, use the table below to calculate how much fabric you will need. This is not such a daunting task as might be imagined and once you have mastered the technique of estimating in this way, you will find it easy to work out how much fabric you require for any counted work.

There are a number of methods you can use to prevent fraying: oversew the edges by hand; machine the edges using a zig-zag stitch; apply a liquid such as 'fray-check', a commercial substance purposely made for this use; or bind the edges with tape (masking tape is not recommended as it can pull threads when being removed and also leave a nasty sticky residue).

Calculating Quantities of Alternative Fabrics

Cross Stitching on Linen over Two Threads
For example: 25 threads per inch linen with design area 100 stitches high x 50 wide. Divide the number of vertical stitches in the design area by the stitch count of the fabric and multiply by 2. This will give you the size of the design area in inches (or millimetres). Repeat this procedure for the horizontal stitches.
Thus:

$$\frac{100}{25} = 4 \times 2 = 8\text{in (205mm)}$$

$$\frac{50}{25} = 2 \times 2 = 4\text{in (100mm)}$$

So the design area is 8 x 4in (205 x 100mm). Add 4-6in (100-150mm) for finishing and the fabric required is 12 x 8in (300 x 205mm)

Cross Stitching on 'Block' Fabrics such as Aida or Over One Thread of Linen
For example: 10-count Aida with design area 100 stitches high x 50 wide. Divide the number of vertical stitches in the design area by the stitch count of the fabric and this will give you the size of the design area in inches (or millimetres). Repeat this procedure for the horizontal stitches.
Thus:

$$\frac{100}{10} = 10\text{in (255mm)}$$

$$\frac{50}{10} = 5\text{in (130mm)}$$

So the design area is 10 x 5in (255 x 130mm). Add 4-6in (100-150mm) for finishing and the fabric required is 14 x 9in (355 x 230mm)

Finding the Centre of the Fabric

Fold the fabric in half and half again and crease lightly. Baste (tack) along these lines in a contrasting sewing thread. The exact centre of the fabric is where the lines cross. Most instructions suggest that you start work here. This is to ensure that your work is evenly distributed and will eliminate any possibility of working off the edge of the fabric. If you particularly want to start at, say, the top left-hand corner of the design, you must calculate carefully where to start by deducting the design size from your fabric size and positioning accordingly. For example, if your fabric size is 12 x 10in (305 x 255mm) and your design size 8 x 6in (205

x 150mm), you will have 4in (100mm) of spare fabric. You should therefore measure 2in (50mm) down from the top edge and 2in (50mm) in from the side edge and begin work here.

Starting to Stitch

Cut your thread no longer than 12-18in (305-460mm). If you are using stranded cotton, separate and untwist all six strands before selecting the number of strands required. This is necessary so that the threads lie flatter and give greater coverage.

Never use a knot to begin stitching; knots can pull through and will give a bumpy finish which will ruin the appearance of your work. To begin stitching on previously unworked fabric, bring the needle up through the fabric leaving about an inch (25mm) of thread at the back. Holding this thread in place, work three or four stitches until the trailing thread is caught and secured. When beginning a new thread on fabric which has been previously stitched, simply run the needle through the loops of three or four stitches at the back of the work near to where you wish to begin stitching. Bring the needle up at the required place, and begin. Be careful not to pull stitches tightly. They should sit evenly on the fabric – tension is just as important in embroidery as in knitting. Make sure that all top stitches in cross stitch are in the same direction. This ensures a smooth even finish. If you remember to 'drop' your needle every so often, this will take the twist out of the thread.

Finishing-off your Thread

The method for finishing/securing a thread is much the same as starting. Leaving yourself enough thread to finish, take the needle through to the back of the work. Run the needle through the back loop of three or four stitches and snip the thread off close to the stitching.

Working the Projects

Instructions for working the stitches used in the following projects are given in the Stitch Directory (page 121). This chapter explains how to interpret an embroidery chart, use a hoop or frame, prepare your fabric and get started on working your design. Further skills, such as finishing, mounting and framing a completed piece of embroidery, enlarging or reducing a design and making a hoop frill or a fold-over card, are described at the back of the book. For suppliers of the materials used, refer to Acknowledgements on page 127.

FLOWER GARLAND

*Tiny rose-buds adorn this floral garland, framing an
initial from the Floral Alphabet (pages 54 to 59) The design is
worked in cross stitch over two threads of linen using two
strands of embroidery cotton (floss).*

Design size: 6in (152mm) circumference
Stitch count: 86 × 84

10 × 10in (250 × 250mm) cream evenweave
  linen, 28 threads per inch (25mm)
DMC stranded cottons (floss) shown in the key
8in (203mm) wooden embroidery hoop
For the hoop frill:
54 × 7in (1,372 × 178mm) cream
  cotton fabric

54in (1,372mm) of 1½in (40mm) cream lace
  with eyelet holes
60in (1,524mm) of ⅛in (4mm) peach satin
  ribbon
30in (762mm) of ¼in (7mm) peach, cream
  and pale-green satin ribbon
Small peach-coloured satin rose bud

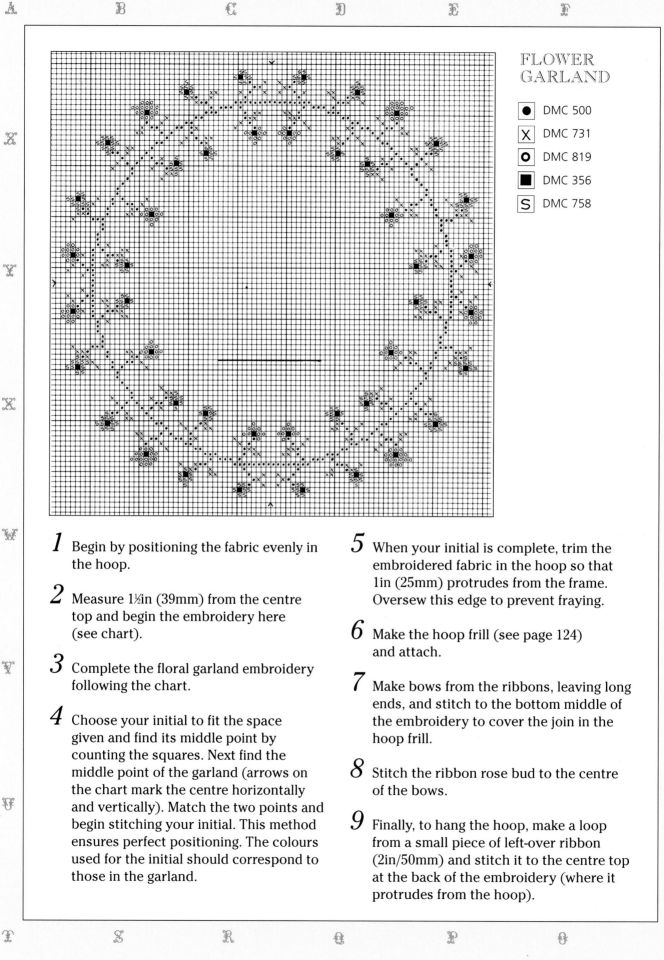

FLOWER
GARLAND

- ● DMC 500
- X DMC 731
- ○ DMC 819
- ■ DMC 356
- S DMC 758

1 Begin by positioning the fabric evenly in the hoop.

2 Measure 1½in (39mm) from the centre top and begin the embroidery here (see chart).

3 Complete the floral garland embroidery following the chart.

4 Choose your initial to fit the space given and find its middle point by counting the squares. Next find the middle point of the garland (arrows on the chart mark the centre horizontally and vertically). Match the two points and begin stitching your initial. This method ensures perfect positioning. The colours used for the initial should correspond to those in the garland.

5 When your initial is complete, trim the embroidered fabric in the hoop so that 1in (25mm) protrudes from the frame. Oversew this edge to prevent fraying.

6 Make the hoop frill (see page 124) and attach.

7 Make bows from the ribbons, leaving long ends, and stitch to the bottom middle of the embroidery to cover the join in the hoop frill.

8 Stitch the ribbon rose bud to the centre of the bows.

9 Finally, to hang the hoop, make a loop from a small piece of left-over ribbon (2in/50mm) and stitch it to the centre top at the back of the embroidery (where it protrudes from the hoop).

MINIATURE SAMPLER IN CANDLE-SCREEN

This charming little sampler is quick and easy to work in cross stitch using only four colours. Use two strands of cotton (floss) over two threads of linen.

Design size: 4⅝ × 3⅛in (117 × 80mm)
Stitch count: 81 × 55

7 × 6in (178 × 152mm) unbleached
 Edinburgh linen, 36 threads per inch
 (25mm)
DMC stranded cottons (floss): 823, 918,
 676, 732
Small candle-screen

1 Find the centre of the design and work from this point outwards following the chart.

2 When complete, fit the embroidery into the candle-screen, following the manufacturer's instructions.

Alternatives

1 Add a mount and frame as a conventional picture.

2 Enlarge the design by working on a linen with less threads per inch (25mm), or adding a simple border.

3 Enlarge and work the design in bright colours on a white or cream fabric. Choose a brightly coloured frame suitable for a child's bedroom.

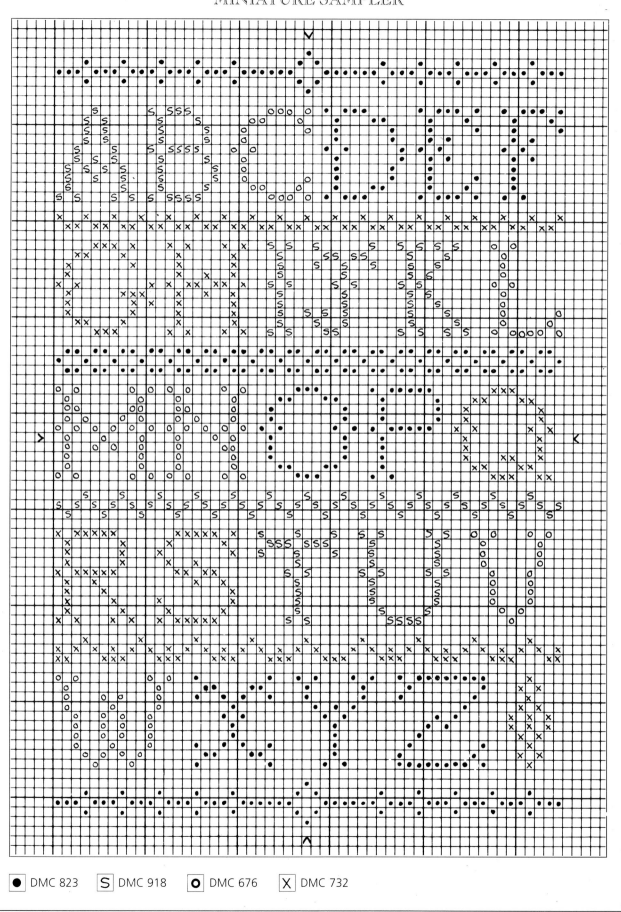

● DMC 823   S DMC 918   O DMC 676   X DMC 732

A CELEBRATION OF MARRIAGE

A delightful gift for a newly married couple, this design (overleaf) is quick and easy to make. The initials used are the same as the Alphabet with Flourishes design, but they look so different worked in a pastel colour with silver. The charming frame echoes and complements the shape of the design.
The design is worked in cross stitch and back stitch over two threads of fabric, using two strands of embroidery cotton (floss). Use the silver thread intact – do not separate the strands.

Design size: 4¾ × 4¾ (120 × 120mm)

12 × 8in (305 × 205mm) white evenweave fabric, 25 threads per inch (25mm). (This allows sufficient fabric to frame the piece as shown.)
DMC stranded cotton (floss) 813
DMC silver thread D283
Approximately 6in (150mm) narrow white ribbon
Purchased wooden frame and card mount

1 Measure 3in (75mm) from the bottom of the fabric lengthways. This will be the base line for the embroidery.

2 Work out the date required *in pencil* on graph paper using the numerals from the Traditional Alphabet sampler chart on pages 102–3. Find the mid-point of the bottom line of your date and position this at the mid-point of the base line. This then gives the position from which all the rest of the embroidery is worked.

3 Following the chart, work the '&' symbol (the flourishes are worked in back stitch using DMC silver D283), the birds and the heart. The strings holding the heart are worked in back stitch with two

strands of DMC 813 and one strand of DMC silver D283.

4 Choose your initials from the Alphabet with Flourishes chart on pages 20–21 and position them on the line shown on the main chart, ie either side of the '&' symbol. Work the flourishes in back stitch, DMC silver D283.

5 When the embroidery is complete, make a small bow from the ribbon and attach in the position shown with small invisible stitches in a matching thread.

6 Mount your embroidery on the card provided (if using the frame shown) or simply stretch, mount and frame as normal.

Alternatives

1 Use the design for a wedding card.

2 Use the design for a small cushion edged with a white lace frill. (This could be used as the ring cushion during the wedding ceremony.)

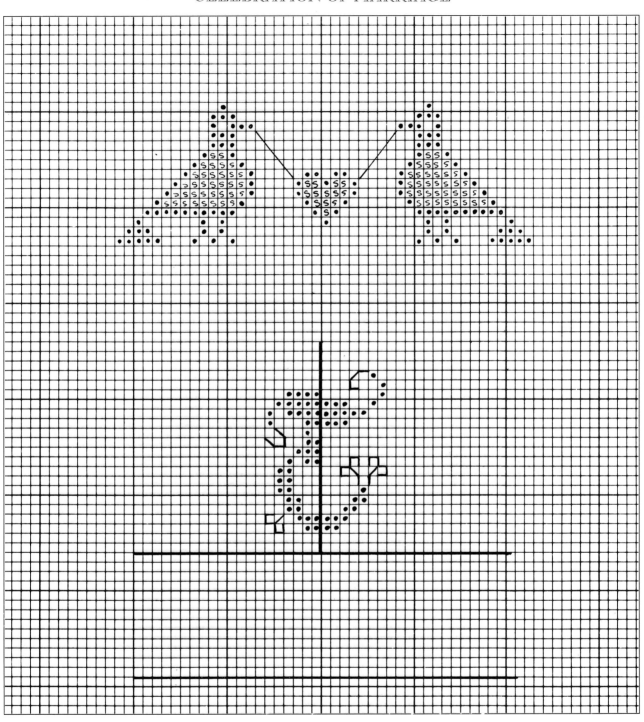

● DMC 813

S D283 (silver)

A Celebration of Marriage

ALPHABET WITH FLOURISHES

This is one of my favourite alphabets and is based on an old and very popular alphabet often found on Scottish samplers. The main body of the initial is worked in cross stitch over two threads of linen using two strands of embroidery cotton (floss). The flourishes are worked in back stitch over two threads of linen in DMC gold thread. A selection of initials is here shown on trinket pots and a paper-weight.

For the E: cream evenweave linen, 28 threads per inch (25mm)

For the L,B,I and H; cream evenweave linen, 25 threads per inch (25mm)

Purchased porcelain trinket pots

Purchased paper-weight

Stranded cottons (floss) in your own choice of colours

DMC gold thread D282

For the H: Designer silk 405 and DMC silver thread D283

1 To estimate how much fabric you need, measure the diameter of your chosen pot or paper-weight and add 3in (75mm) all the way round. This will allow enough fabric to fit a 4in (100mm) embroidery frame which is a perfect size to use for working small projects like this.

2 Position your initial in the centre of your fabric and, beginning at the middle point, work the initial following the chart.

3 Make up the trinket pots or paper-weight following the manufacturer's instructions.

Alternatives

1 Work the whole alphabet in black and gold and add a blackwork border (page 45). This would make a superb sampler.

2 Work a name from the initials, then frame or make up as a cushion.

3 Work just one initial, then add a couple of mounts and a beautiful frame.

Selection of initials from the Alphabet with Flourishes, made up into trinket pots and a paper-weight

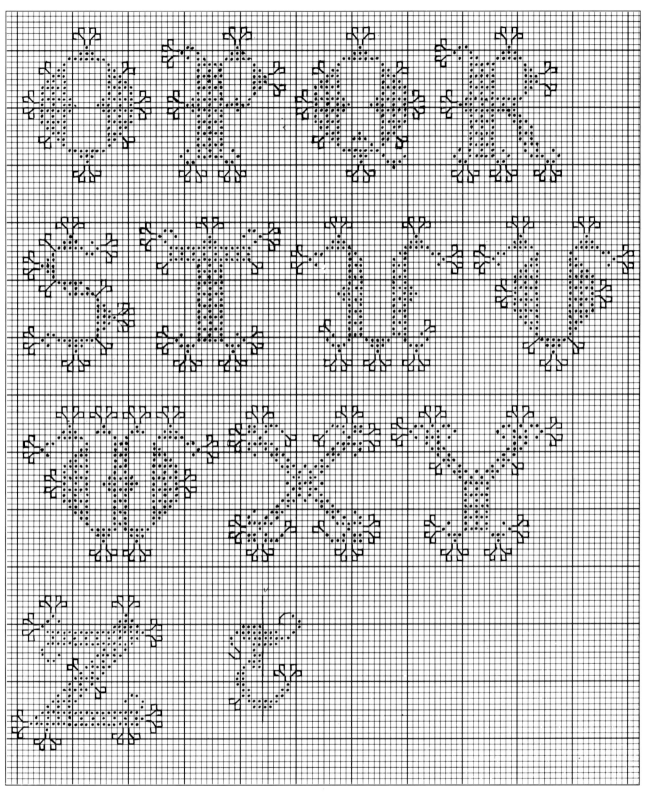

MEDIEVAL INITIALS

Rich and vibrant, this canvaswork initial is reminiscent of the opulent embroidery of the Middle Ages.

Design size: 4 × 4in (100 × 100mm)

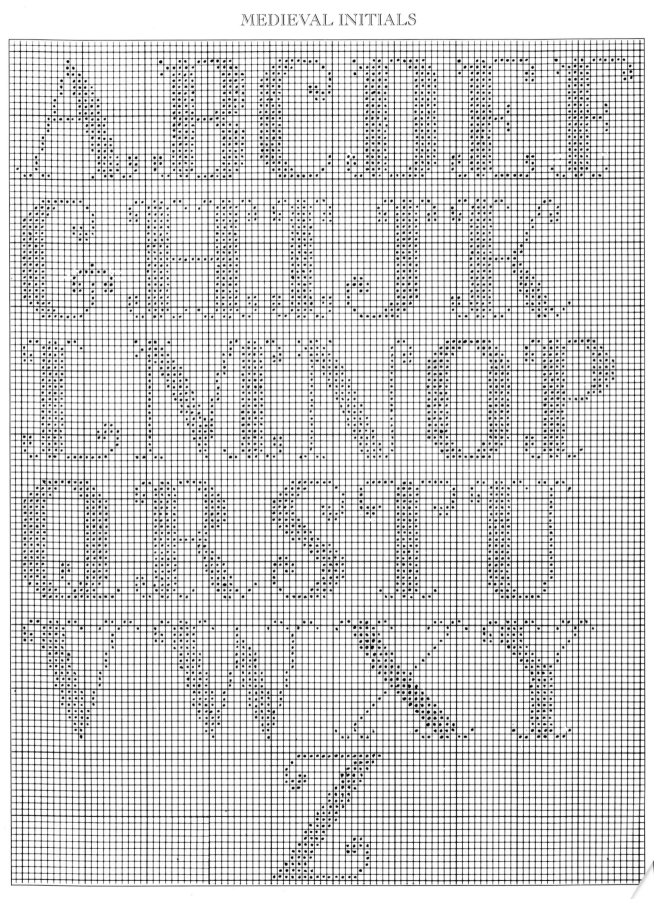

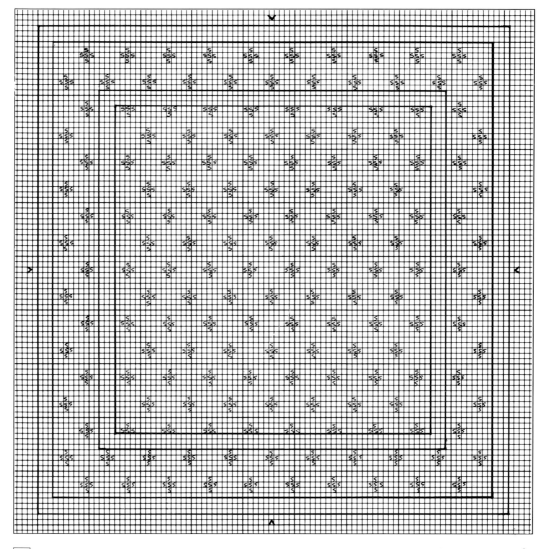

S DMC 676	Paterna Persian Yarn A211 (inner background and border)	Paterna Persian Yarn A922 (outer background and border)	(DMC gold D282 for body of initial, DMC 823 for outline of initial)

7 × 7in (178 × 178mm) white petit-point
  22-count canvas
DMC gold thread D282
DMC stranded cotton (floss) as shown in the key
Paterna Persian wool yarn as shown in the key

1 Choose your initial from the alphabet chart and position it in the centre of the canvas.

2 Beginning at the middle point, work your initial in cross stitch over two threads of canvas in gold thread. Outline in tent stitch DMC 823 stranded cotton using two strands over one thread.

3 Fill in the remaining background from the chart given, using one strand of wool and two strands of embroidery cotton as indicated in the key.

4 The borders are worked in satin stitch over two threads using one strand of wool.

5 If you wish, frame your work with a velvet-covered mount.

GAELIC ALPHABET SAMPLER

Although only three colours are used in this easy-to-work sampler (overleaf), the use of a variegated thread adds interest and results in a stunning design. The Gaelic alphabet has only eighteen letters. The words 'Mo Dhachaidh Milis' mean 'My Sweet Home'. The alphabet and pictorial scene are both worked over two threads of Floba. The words are worked over one thread only. Use one strand of perlé cotton throughout.

Design size: 11½ × 13in (293 × 330mm)
Stitch count: 98 × 109

16 × 17in (410 × 430mm) natural Floba, 18 threads per inch (25mm)
DMC perlé cottons: 823, 730, 115

1 Find the centre of the design on the chart, match to the centre of the fabric and work from this point outwards.

2 When you have finished working the alphabet and pictorial scene, position the first letter of the words as shown on the main chart. Remembering to work over one thread only, complete the words using the additional chart.

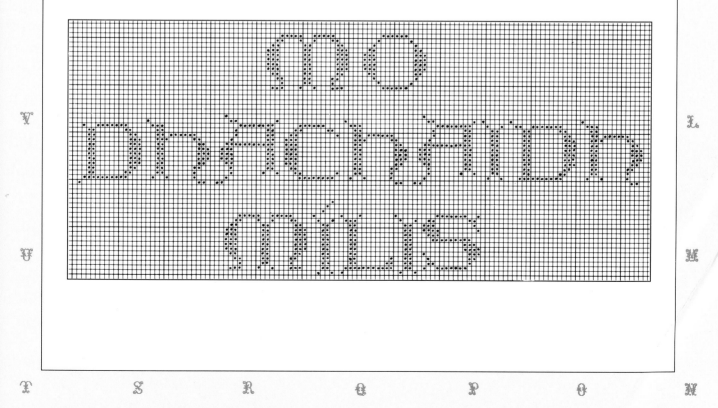

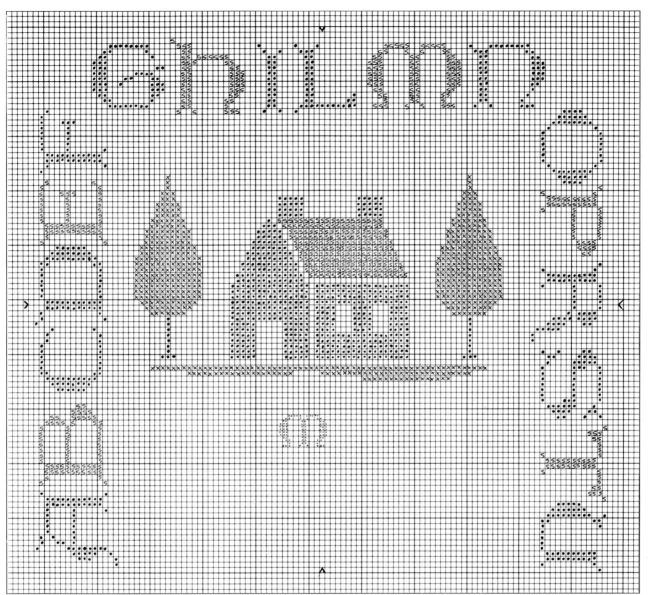

DMC PERLÉ COTTON

 823

S | 115

X | 730

Words 823

Gaelic Alphabet Sampler

WELSH SAMPLER

This beautiful sampler is worked on a soft beige Aida fabric in space-dyed linen thread, using only two different colours. It is worked in cross stitch and back stitch over one block of fabric using one strand of linen thread.

Design size: 8 × 10½in (205 × 267mm)
Stitch count: 108 × 147

12 × 15in (305 × 380mm) beige 14-count Aida fabric
Variegated linen embroidery thread from Brethyn Brith in blue/grey and beige/brown (or DMC variegated stranded cotton floss 91 and 105. Use two strands if using this alternative)

Find the centre of the design, match to the centre of the fabric and work from this point outwards, using varying lengths of each thread, alternately, to achieve the desired effect.

Alternative

This design could be worked in stranded cotton (floss) using one or more colours.

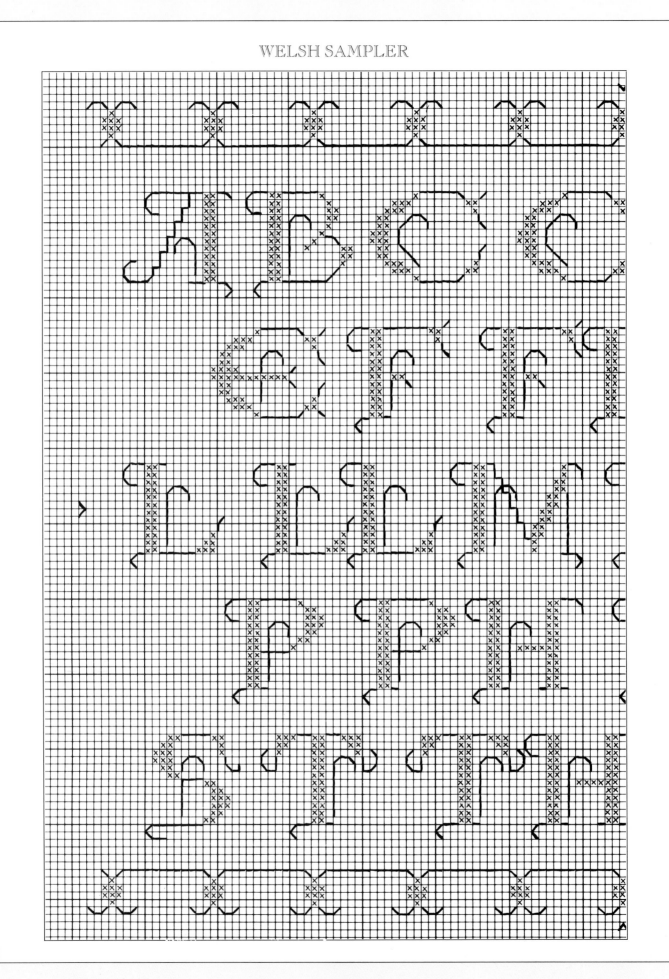

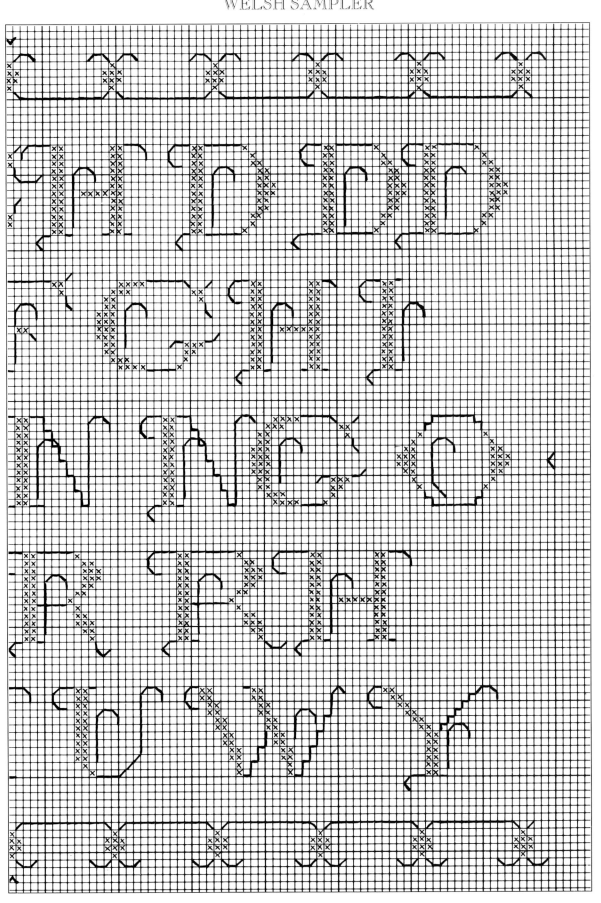

QUILTED FLORENTINE INITIALS

Florentine embroidery (satin stitch in a flame pattern - also known as Bargello, flame stitch, cushion stitch and Hungary stitch) is used in this project as a background, leaving the actual initial unworked (as in Assisi initials). The initial itself and the completed background are then quilted to give an unusual and charming look to this pretty pastel piece.

Design size: 4 × 3¼in (100 × 83mm)

10 × 10in (255 × 255mm) cream evenweave
  linen, 25 threads per inch (25mm)
German Flower Threads: 3303, 2096,
  3532, 3305
10 × 10in (255 × 255mm) piece polyester
  wadding
10 × 10in (255 × 255mm) piece white
  cotton fabric
White sewing cotton for outlining initial
  and quilting
8in (205mm) embroidery hoop

1 Choose your initial from the Quilted Florentine Alphabet chart, positioning it in the centre of the linen and, using back stitch, outline in one strand of white sewing cotton.

2 Using satin stitch, fill in the background from the chart on page 33, leaving the letter unworked.

3 Lay the completed embroidery right side uppermost over the polyester wadding and then place both of these layers over the piece of white cotton.

4 Make large tacking stitches through all layers to hold in position.

5 Place the stitched layers in the embroidery hoop then back stitch through all the layers, outlining first the initial and then the Florentine background.

Alternatives

1 Enlarge the initial and then work it on a piece of linen large enough to make a cushion, extending the background to fit. Make a frill to match one of the colours in the background, then add a line of piping to match one of the other colours.

2 Work the design in bright colours in shiny threads, then mount it, using a card with a ready-made aperture.

*(above) Quilted Florentine Initial;
(below) Florentine background*

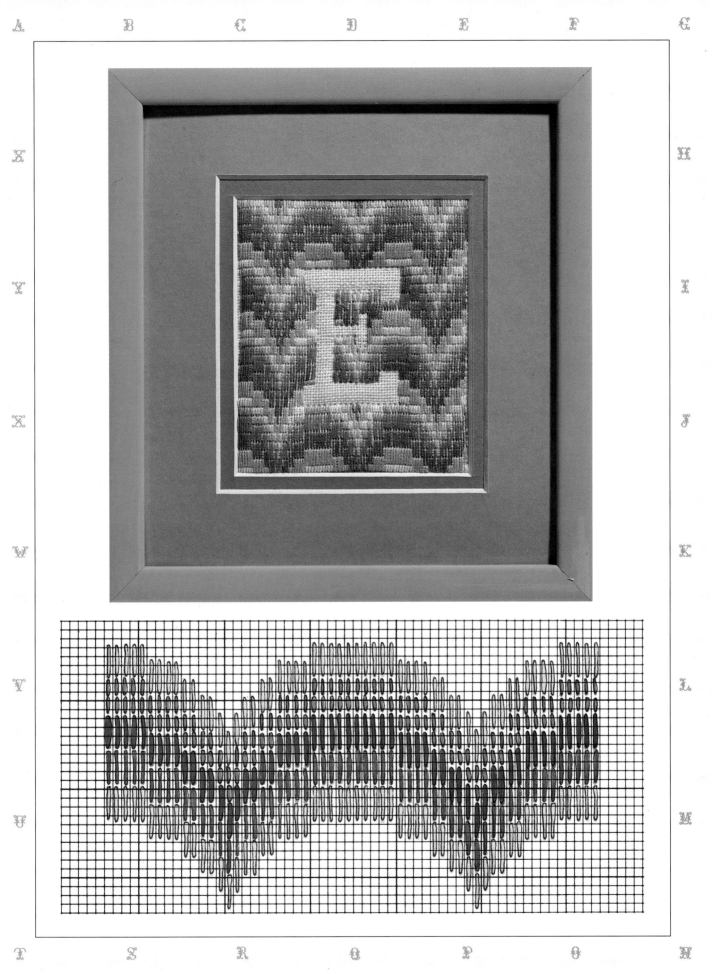

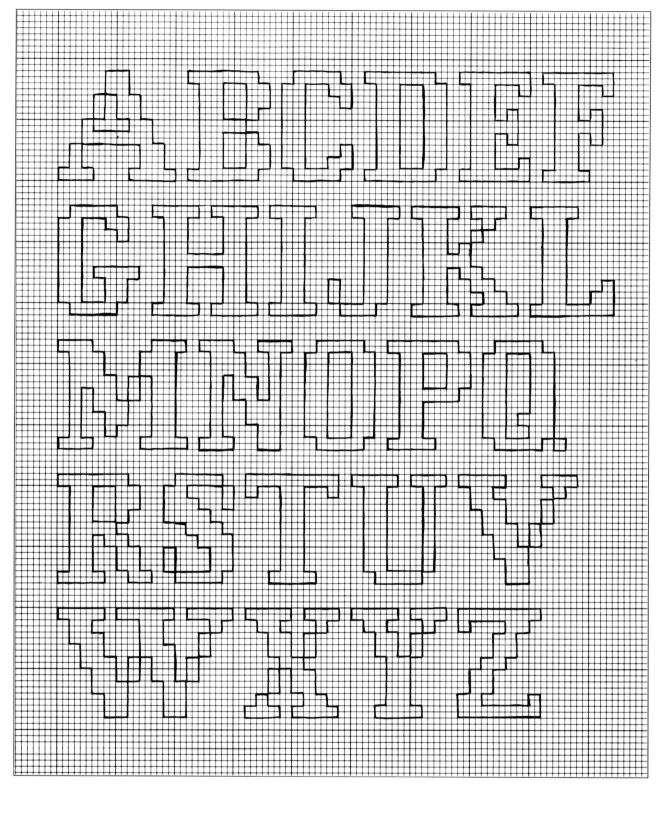

THE CATHERINE DARCY SAMPLER

The Catherine Darcy sampler (pages 38–9), worked in shades of cream and white in a wide variety of threads on a cream linen base, is destined to become a family heirloom. Work it as shown, with the name and date given, as a reproduction sampler, or personalise it with your own details for your family to treasure. This design is worked in cross stitch, eyelet stitch, back stitch and satin stitch. The pulled-thread effect is achieved using some of these stitches. The rich 'brocade' effect of the border is achieved by working cross stitch in perlé cotton, then edging it using back stitch and silver thread.

Design size: 8¾ × 8¾in (220mm × 220mm)
Stitch count: 133 × 133

13 × 13in (330 × 330mm) cream evenweave linen, 32 threads per inch (25mm)
Stranded cottons (floss), German flower thread, Marlitt viscose thread, rayonne à broder, perlé cotton, Zwicky pure silk thread and DMC silver thread D283 (see chart key for numbers)

1 Find the centre of the design, match to the centre of the fabric and work from this point outwards, following the chart. Eyelet stitch is used in the row under letters A-H and for the flowers on either side of the middle row, lower case W-Z Under I-Q, work two satin stitches vertically and pull tight to give the pulled-thread effect. Under R-Y work satin stitches in the same way but horizontally, and interspersed with cross stitches. Satin stitch is also used for the two triangular central rows and the white flowers. Elsewhere, use cross stitch. Edge the cross-stitch border with back stitch in silver.

2 If you wish to substitute your own name and date, chart these details on graph paper, using the alphabets and numerals given in this sampler. Position them as shown on the chart.

CATHERINE DARCY SAMPLER

DMC COTTON PERLÉ

X Ecru

● 543

DMC STRANDED COTTON (FLOSS)

S Ecru (3 strands)

O 842

DMC RAYONNE À BRODER

■ 4746 (1 strand)

I B5200 (1 strand) and satin stitch flowers

ZWICKY PURE SILK

2134 (2 strands) Eyelet stitches under letters A–H

2330 (2 strands) Vertical 'pulled' satin stitch under letters I–Q

2330 (2 strands) Horizontal 'pulled' satin stitch under letters R–Y

2330 (2 strands) Satin stitch triangular rows above and below lower case alphabet

V German Flower Thread: White (2 strands)

Z Designer Silk 803 (1 strand)

/ Marlitt 1012 (2 strands)

DMC Silver D283 (back stitch edging to border)

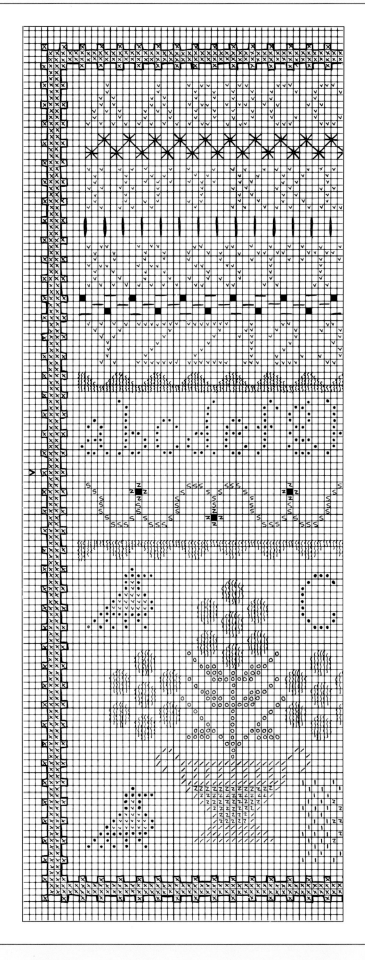

WHITEWORK VASE

The design for this simple whitework vase was taken from the Catherine Darcy Sampler, using the same chart, and it is effectively displayed in an opaque glass trinket pot. Refer to the chart on page 36 and use the same threads and the same number of strands.

Design size: 2¾ × 2¾in (70 × 70mm)
Stitch count: 41 × 39

7 × 7in (178 × 178mm) cream Belfast linen, 32 threads per inch (25mm)
Threads as shown in the key (page 36)
Opaque glass trinket pot with 4in (100mm) lid

1 Find the centre of the vase section of the design on the chart, match to the centre of the fabric and work from this point outwards.

2 When the embroidery is complete, fit it into the trinket pot lid following the manufacturer's instructions.

The Catherine Darcy Sampler and the Whitework Vase

CONGRATULATIONS BANNER

This cheerful easy-to-make banner will brighten up any special occasion - wedding, christening, birthday or anniversary.
The word 'Congratulations' and the balloons are worked in cross stitch using two strands of embroidery cotton (floss) over two threads of linen. The balloons and their strings are outlined in back stitch using two strands of embroidery cotton.

Design size: 5½ × 17in (140 × 430mm) including fabric edge
Stitch count: 40 × 170

5½ × 17in (140 × 430mm) white evenweave linen, 25 threads per inch (25mm)
DMC stranded cottons (floss) as shown in the key
8 × 19½ (205 × 495mm) grape-coloured cotton
Matching grape-coloured sewing thread
5½ × 17in (140 × 430mm) terylene wadding
30in (765mm) very narrow yellow ribbon
A pair of 9in (230mm) wooden bell pulls

1 Complete the embroidery following the chart and, if necessary, press lightly on the back.

2 Lay the grape-coloured cotton fabric, wrong side up, on a flat surface. Position the terylene wadding centrally on the fabric, then place the embroidery, right side up, on top of the wadding. Measure from the edges of the linen to the edges of the fabric to make sure the embroidery is positioned centrally, then tack all three layers together.

3 Make ½in (12mm) turnings at the top and bottom of the fabric. Turn these edges over the embroidered linen to make a 1in (25mm) turning. Tack. Using the matching sewing thread, machine or hand stitch into place, close to the edge of the fabric.

4 Complete the side edges in the same way, leaving openings at the top and bottom for the wooden rods to be passed through. Press all turnings lightly.

5 Cut the yellow ribbon into four and make four bows. Stitch the bows into place at the corners of the linen, using stitches which do not show.

6 Remove one end from each of the bell pull rods and insert them through the channel at either side of the embroidery, with the finials at the top.

7 The rods in the photograph have been fitted into holes drilled into a piece of wood. An even simpler idea is to cut styrofoam shapes (available from florists) to fit two small plant pots, paint the plant pots in a bright colour to match the embroidery, tie a ribbon round them, finish with a bow, then insert the rods into the styrofoam.

Alternatives

1 Frame the embroidery using several card mounts to match the colours used.

2 Work the embroidery over just one thread of linen and make up as a fold-over card.

3 Make a really big banner by working over four or even six threads of linen (increase strands used accordingly). Finish as advised but instead of displaying on finial posts, sew ribbons to the back to form loops for hanging.

CONGRATULATIONS BANNER

V	DMC 597	C	DMC 744	Z	DMC 813	Balloon outlines and strings DMC black 310	
O	DMC ecru	X	DMC 743	I	DMC 3325		
◢	DMC 926	/	DMC 955	■	DMC 602		
⬟	DMC 3042	S	DMC 954	=	DMC 604		
●	DMC 3041	Λ	DMC 224	L	DMC 223		

STORK INITIALS

What better way to welcome a new baby than to work this pretty stork design. It can be completed quickly and would make an ideal christening gift.
This design is worked in cross stitch using three strands of embroidery cotton (floss) over one block of fabric.

Design size: 8in (205mm), ie the size of the hoop

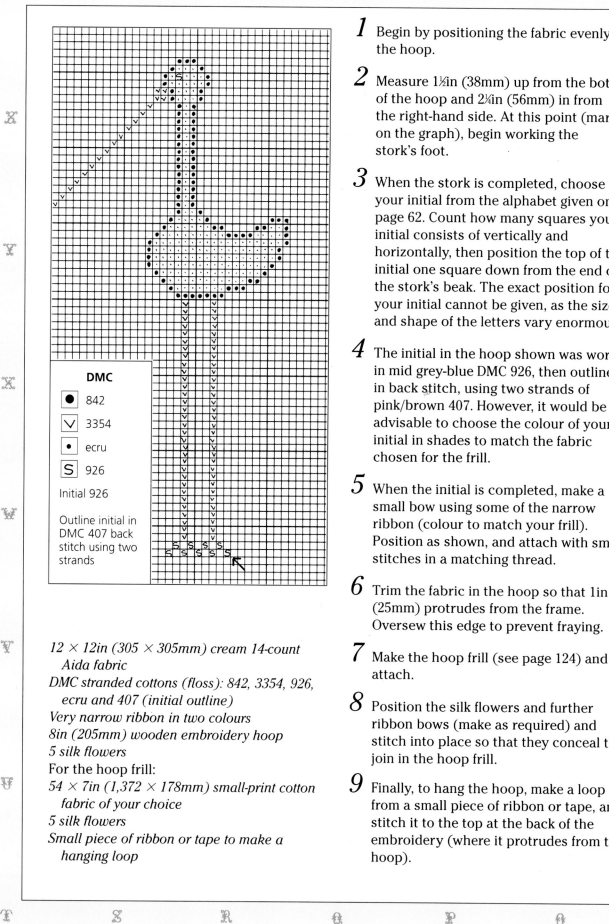

DMC
- ● 842
- V 3354
- · ecru
- S 926

Initial 926

Outline initial in DMC 407 back stitch using two strands

12 × 12in (305 × 305mm) cream 14-count Aida fabric
DMC stranded cottons (floss): 842, 3354, 926, ecru and 407 (initial outline)
Very narrow ribbon in two colours
8in (205mm) wooden embroidery hoop
5 silk flowers
For the hoop frill:
54 × 7in (1,372 × 178mm) small-print cotton fabric of your choice
5 silk flowers
Small piece of ribbon or tape to make a hanging loop

1 Begin by positioning the fabric evenly in the hoop.

2 Measure 1½in (38mm) up from the bottom of the hoop and 2¼in (56mm) in from the right-hand side. At this point (marked on the graph), begin working the stork's foot.

3 When the stork is completed, choose your initial from the alphabet given on page 62. Count how many squares your initial consists of vertically and horizontally, then position the top of the initial one square down from the end of the stork's beak. The exact position for your initial cannot be given, as the size and shape of the letters vary enormously.

4 The initial in the hoop shown was worked in mid grey-blue DMC 926, then outlined in back stitch, using two strands of pink/brown 407. However, it would be advisable to choose the colour of your initial in shades to match the fabric chosen for the frill.

5 When the initial is completed, make a small bow using some of the narrow ribbon (colour to match your frill). Position as shown, and attach with small stitches in a matching thread.

6 Trim the fabric in the hoop so that 1in (25mm) protrudes from the frame. Oversew this edge to prevent fraying.

7 Make the hoop frill (see page 124) and attach.

8 Position the silk flowers and further ribbon bows (make as required) and stitch into place so that they conceal the join in the hoop frill.

9 Finally, to hang the hoop, make a loop from a small piece of ribbon or tape, and stitch it to the top at the back of the embroidery (where it protrudes from the hoop).

ASSISI INITIALS

Assisi is a form of cross stitch embroidery which uses a method known as 'voiding', that is, the background is embroidered instead of the design. In this case the design is an initial, enhanced by a pretty blackwork border.

Design size: 4¼ × 4¼in (110 × 110mm)
Stitch count: 56 × 56

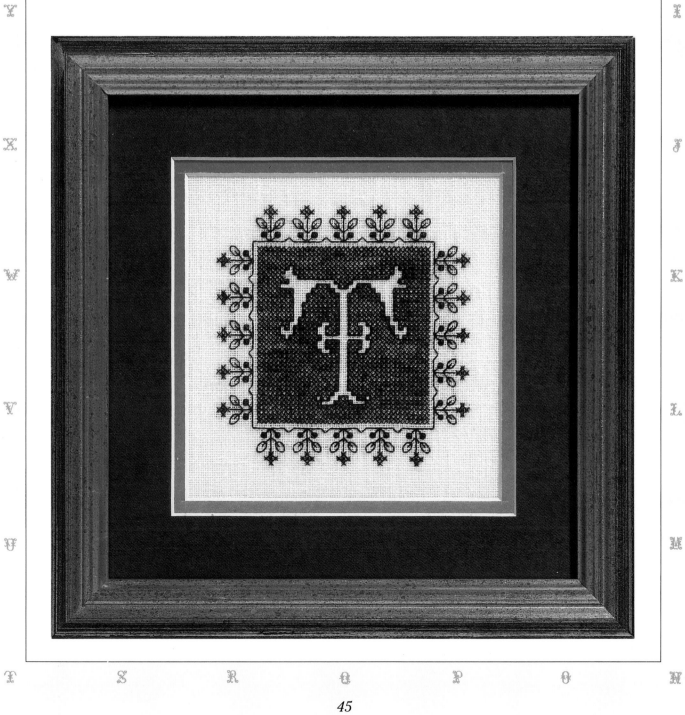

8 × 8in (205 × 205mm) cream evenweave linen, 25 threads per inch (25mm)
DMC stranded cotton (floss): black 310

1 Using the Assisi Alphabet chart choose your initial. Counting the squares on the chart, find the middle of the initial. Centre this on your fabric (to find the middle of your fabric, fold in half then half again). For a W, enlarge the border by one flower.

2 Using two strands of cotton (floss), work the outline of the initial in back stitch over two threads of linen. Fill in the background as shown in the chart above with cross stitch over two threads of linen, making sure that your initial is centred in the middle of the design (arrows mark the centre of the chart vertically and horizontally). You may like to mark the position of your initial lightly in pencil on the main chart to ensure that it is accurately centred.

3 Finally, work the blackwork border in back stitch and cross stitch.

Alternatives

1 Try working the design in a different colour thread or threads. See the Summer Garden Alphabet (page 70) which shows how effective a random placing of colour can be.

2 Enlarge the design by working over four threads instead of two. Work the design in soft cotton (floss) in bold colours on a fabric such as Floba for a cushion.

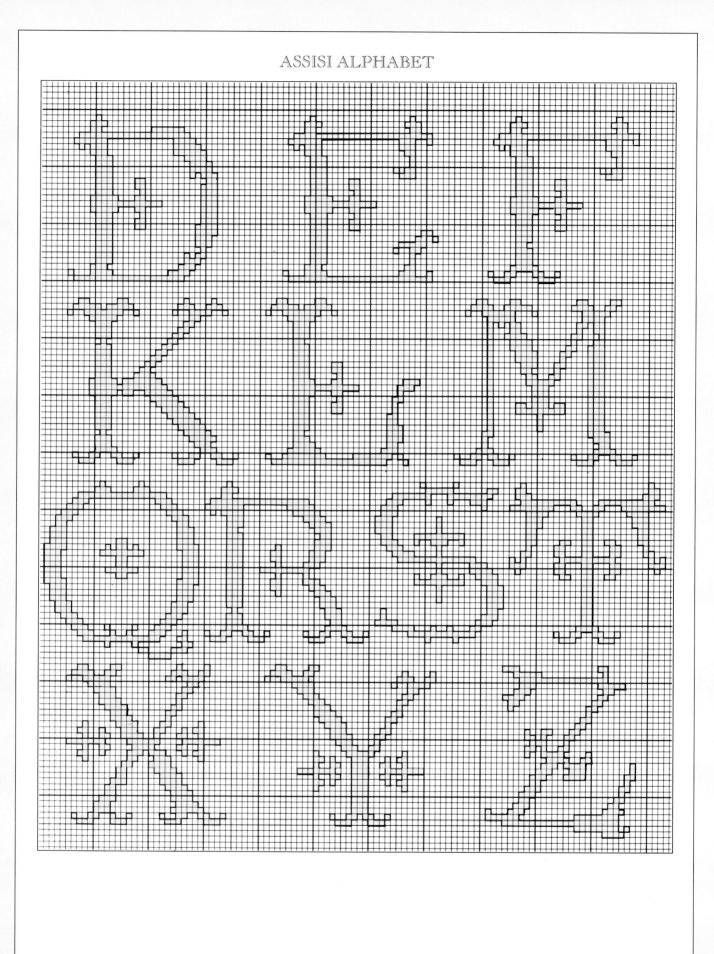

THE 'LOVING EYE' SAMPLER AND BOOKMARK

The words to this charming verse appear on the side of a building (now a restaurant) in Keswick in the Lake District, England. They immediately conjured up for me the wonderful contribution made throughout the ages by the embroiderer's 'loving eye and patient hand'. The sampler (overleaf) is worked in cross stitch and back stitch over two threads of linen, using two strands of embroidery cotton (floss). The bookmark uses a section of the sampler's pretty cross stitch border.

Design size: 6½ × 10in (165 × 250mm)
Stitch count: 99 × 145

10½ × 14in (265 × 356mm) cream evenweave linen, 28 threads per inch (25mm)
DMC stranded cottons (floss) as shown in the key
Purchased bookmark

Find the centre of the design on the sampler chart and the fabric and work from this point outwards following the chart. Work the back stitch letters in DMC 3371. For the bookmark, work a section of the sampler border, in cross stitch, following the chart key.

(overleaf) The 'Loving Eye' Sampler and Bookmark

LOVING EYE SAMPLER

●	DMC 3371	S	DMC 890	M	DMC 3685
X	DMC 733	=	DMC 356	O	DMC 3779

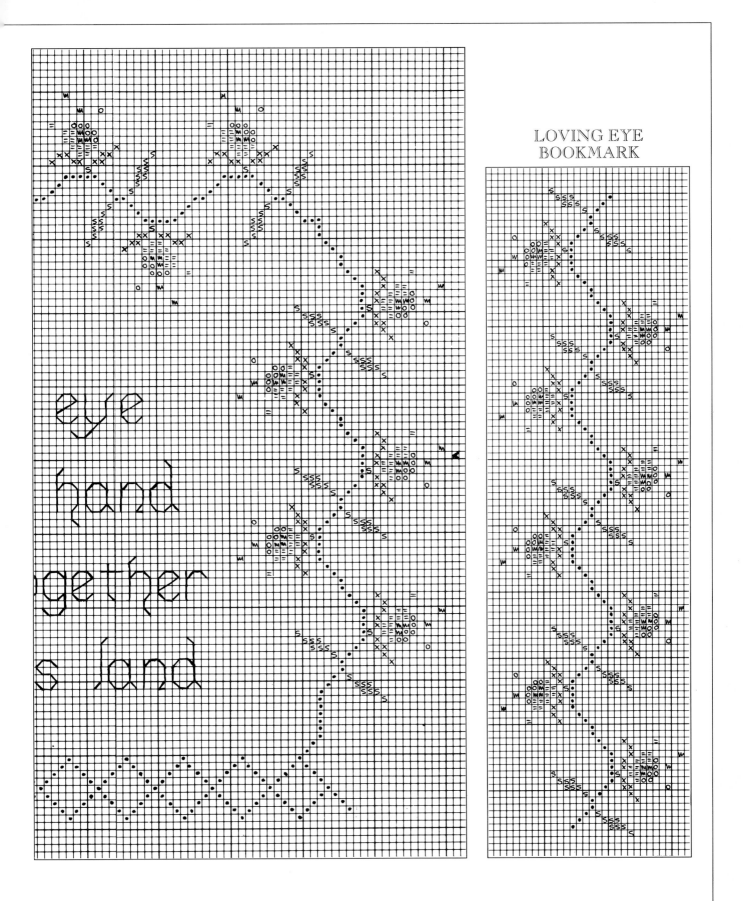

LOVING EYE
BOOKMARK

eye

hand

together

s land

FLORAL ALPHABET

This pretty alphabet in pastel shades can be used to great effect for a variety of projects that are quick and easy to make. Work the whole alphabet to create an impressive sampler, or choose an initial and frame it in an original way. This alphabet co-ordinates beautifully with the Alphabet Border initials shown on page 62. Try using one of the Floral Alphabet letters as your capital and complete a name with the Alphabet Border lower case letters.

Design size: 11¼ × 13¾in (285 × 350mm)
Stitch count: 157 × 191

THE SAMPLER

16 × 18in (410 × 460mm) cream evenweave linen, 28 threads per inch (25mm)
DMC stranded cottons (floss): 926, 316, 890, 818

This design is worked in cross stitch over two threads of linen using two strands of embroidery cotton. Find the centre of the design on the chart and fabric and work from this point outwards.

Floral Alphabet Sampler with 'Amy' and 'Laura' and Initial H

FLORAL
ALPHABET

DMC

●	926
O	316
X	890
V	818

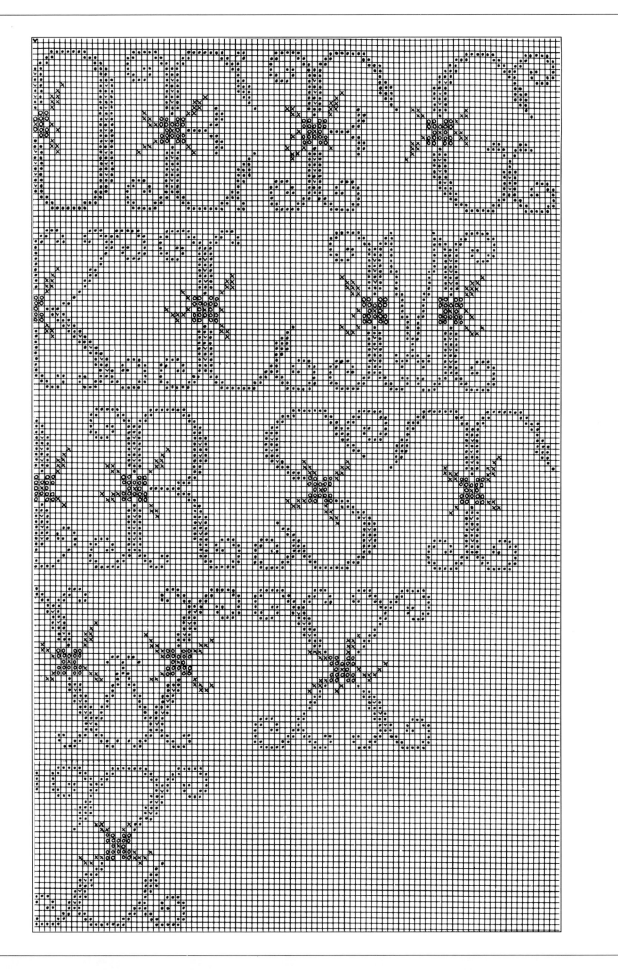

INITIAL BROOCH AND PENDANT

This brooch and pendant (opposite) show a charming way of using the embroidered initials from the Floral Alphabet, which has been reduced in size by working tent stitch over just one thread, with two strands of embroidery cotton (floss). Many of the cross stitch alphabets could be used in this way.

Small pieces of cream evenweave linen: 25 threads per inch (25mm) for the small oval brooch and 32 threads per inch (25mm) for the pendant

DMC stranded cottons (floss): for the pendant; as for the sampler; For the brooch, worked in the reverse colourway, ie pink in place of blue/blue in place of pink

Purchased brooch and pendant

1 Check the stitch count of your chosen initial. For advice on estimating the size your initial will be, refer to the section on using alternative fabrics (page 10)

2 Position your initials, and work them in tent stitch using two strands over one thread of linen.

3 When the embroidery is complete, make up the brooch and pendant following the manufacturer's instructions.

Examples of further uses for the Floral Alphabet

'Amy' (page 54) was worked in cross stitch on 14 count white Aida reversing the colours given in the key, ie, pink in place of blue, blue in place of pink. Two strands of embroidery cotton (floss) were used over one block of fabric. The leaves were worked in the same colours as shown in the key. The hoop frill was made from a cotton print fabric, white lace, ribbon bows and silk flowers.

'Laura' (page 54) was worked in cross stitch on 14-count Yorkshire Aida 440, using Designer silk No 703 grey/black/brown, one strand over one block of fabric. The hoop frill was made from a cotton print fabric, cream cotton lace and ribbon bows.

The initial M (opposite) was worked in cross stitch over two threads of cream evenweave linen, 28 threads per inch (25mm) in colours as shown in the key. The hoop frill was made from cotton print fabric, cream cotton lace, ribbon bows, a small bunch of dried flowers and one silk flower.

The initial H (page 54) was worked in cross stitch over two threads of cream evenweave linen, 28 threads per inch (25mm), in the alternate pink colourway described above, then framed in a 4in (110mm) round brass frame. A 30in (765mm) piece of cream lace was gathered and glued into place on the back of the frame, using impact adhesive.

The initial B (opposite) shown as a pincushion was worked in cross stitch over two threads of cream evenweave linen, 32 threads per inch (25mm), in the alternate pink colourway (as above for 'Amy'). The wooden pincushion base is readily available from many needlecraft stores.

To make up such a pincushion, when the embroidery is complete, trim the fabric to form a circle. Run a gathering thread approximately ½in (10mm) from the edge of the circle. Unscrew the padded fabric centre from the wooden surround. Cover, centralising the initial, then pull in the gathers and secure firmly. Either glue or stitch a 12in (305mm) length of narrow lace around the edge so that it is half concealed. Replace the centre by screwing it back into the wooden base.

The initial K (opposite) is shown displayed in a small gold frame. It was worked in cross stitch over two threads of cream evenweave linen, 32 threads per inch (25mm) in colours as shown in the main key.

The initial V is shown displayed in a small card with a heart-shaped aperture. The fabric used is 18-count cream Aida. The design was stitched in cross stitch using two strands of embroidery cotton (floss) over one block of fabric. The reverse pink colourway was used and the leaves were worked in a mid sage-green.

ALPHABET BORDER SAMPLER

An unusual border of stylish lower case letters frames this initial from the Floral Alphabet. Worked in only three colours on a warm-pink Aida fabric, this delightful little sampler would make an ideal gift for a child. The design is worked in cross stitch and back stitch over one block of fabric using two strands of embroidery cotton (floss).

Design size: 9 × 7in (230 × 178mm)
Stitch count: 127 × 96

13 × 11in (330 × 280mm) pink 14-count
 Aida fabric
DMC stranded cottons (floss): 926 (letters),
 223 (heart centres), 818 (outer edges of
 hearts), 926 (back stitch)

1 Choose your initial from the Floral Alphabet chart on pages 56–7 and position in the centre of the Alphabet Border Sampler chart. (Count the number of squares in your initial, find the centre and match up with the centre of the main chart. You may like to mark the position of your initial lightly in pencil on this chart to ensure accurate positioning.)

2 Match the centre of the chart to the centre of the fabric and stitch the initial first.

3 When the initial has been completed work the rest of the design, following the Alphabet Border Sampler chart.

Alternatives

1 Use reverse colours – ie, pink letters on a blue background.

2 Instead of an initial, work a child's full name, date of birth etc, using a smaller alphabet (eg, the Christmas Alphabet, page 116).

Examples of Further Uses for the Alphabet Border Initials

'Anna' was worked in cross stitch on blue Aida fabric 503, using Designer silk No 703 grey/black/brown, over one block of fabric. The hoop frill was made using a 4in (100mm) wooden embroidery hoop, unbleached linen, 36 threads per inch (25mm), a small bunch of dried flowers, a ribbon bow and a ribbon loop. For longer names, simply use a larger hoop.

'Emma' was worked in cross stitch on cream evenweave linen, 32 threads per inch (25mm) using DMC 926 grey/blue stranded cotton (floss) over two threads of linen. The finished embroidery was mounted on a 4½in (115mm) circle of strong card and framed with a 6½in (165mm) painted wicker hoop. Straight pins were used to secure the covered card to the hoop. A small bunch of dried flowers and a ribbon bow were glued to the hoop, using impact adhesive.

BOOKMARKS

Here are three examples (overleaf) of how you can use alphabets or initials to make personalised bookmarks. Most of the alphabets in this book can be used in a similar way, giving plenty of scope for your own ideas.

NICHOLAS BOOKMARK

9 × 2¾in (230 × 70mm) black 14-count Aida
Variegated blue/grey linen thread from
  Brethyn Brith (or DMC variegated stranded
  cotton 91)

1 Work out your chosen name *in pencil* on graph paper using the alphabet on page 110.

2 To centralise your design on the fabric, find the mid point of your name by counting the squares on the graph, then find the mid point of the bookmark by folding in half then half again. Match these two points and begin stitching at the centre in cross stitch using one strand of thread (or two if using DMC) over one block of fabric.

3 When the embroidery is complete, fray the sides of the fabric as shown (9 blocks top and bottom, and 3 blocks at the sides).

KATIE BOOKMARK

Purchased bookmark
DMC variegated stranded cotton (floss) 48

This design is worked in cross stitch using two strands of embroidery cotton over one block of fabric using the Medieval Alphabet, page 23. Follow stages 1 and 2 for 'Nicholas'.

INITIAL 'A' BOOKMARK

9in (230mm) ivory 'linen band', 30 threads
  per inch (25mm)
Stranded cottons (floss) as shown on French
  Alphabet chart key, page 94
4 × ¾in (102 × 20mm) white lace

1 Choose your initial from the French Alphabet chart.

2 Measure 1¾in (45mm) from the bottom of the linen band (this is the base line for stitching). Count the number of squares across the width of your initial, to find its mid point (on the bottom line of the initial). Match this to the mid point of the base line and begin stitching here, using two strands of cotton (floss) over one thread of linen.

3 When your embroidery is complete, hem the top of the band in matching cotton (floss). Hem the bottom of the band then attach the lace to the top line of the hem, at the front, using running stitch, and turning in the raw edges at the sides and slightly gathering as you stitch.

(overleaf) Three bookmarks

ILLUMINATED INITIAL - PSALM 23

This adaptation of a favourite psalm features an illuminated T in the Medieval style. It is worked on Belfast linen in subtle colours and gold thread and is sure to become a treasured heirloom. The example shown has been stitched in tent stitch, but instructions are also given for working some of this design in cross stitch.

Design size: 7¼ × 11in (185 × 280mm)

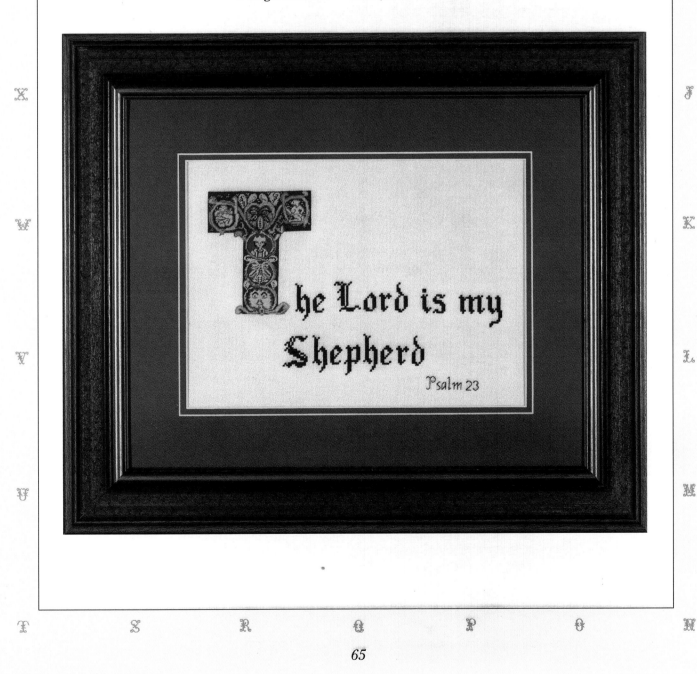

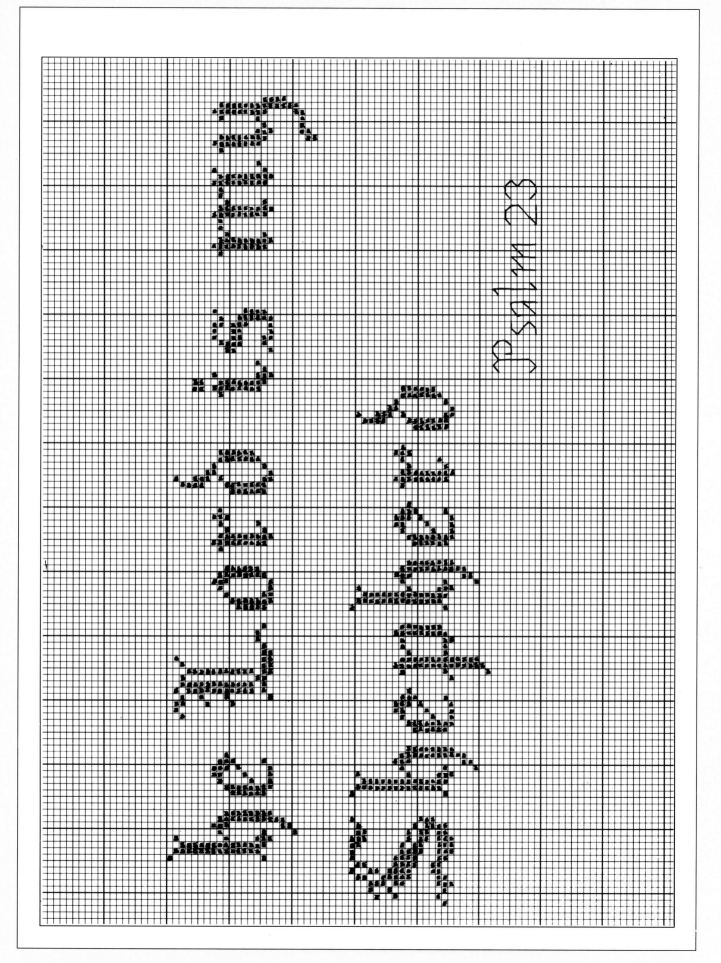

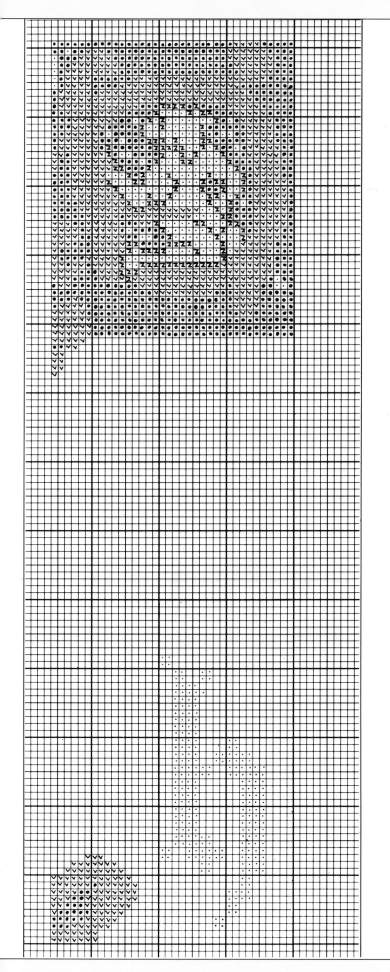

*12 × 16in (305 × 406mm) cream Belfast
linen, 32 threads per inch (25mm)
DMC stranded cottons (floss) as shown in
the key
DMC gold thread D282*

1 Measure 2½ (63mm) down from the top of the linen and 2⅜in (63mm) in from the left-hand side. Begin stitching the top left corner of the illuminated initial in tent stitch, using two strands of embroidery cotton (floss) over one thread of linen. (NB As tent stitch tends to distort fabric, it is recommended that you work this design on a frame.)

2 When you have completed the initial, work the remaining words from the chart using two strands in *either* tent stitch over one thread with each symbol on the chart equal to a block of four tent stitches, *or* in cross stitch over two threads with each symbol equal to one cross stitch. (The example shown has been worked in tent stitch over a block of four.)

3 Finally, complete the words, Psalm 23 in back stitch using two strands of embroidery cotton (floss) over two threads of linen.

ILLUMINATED INITIAL

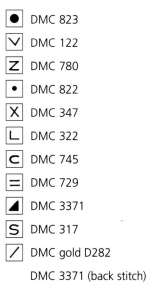

● DMC 823

V DMC 122

Z DMC 780

• DMC 822

X DMC 347

L DMC 322

C DMC 745

= DMC 729

◢ DMC 3371

S DMC 317

/ DMC gold D282

　DMC 3371 (back stitch)

SUMMER GARDEN ALPHABET

This design brings to mind lazy summer days in flower-filled gardens. The Assisi Alphabet used here is the same as for the Assisi Initials (page 45) but the result looks totally different. This project is ideal for using up all those annoying leftover lengths of thread.

For initial shown: 7in × 7in (178 × 178mm) cream evenweave linen, 28 threads per inch (25mm)
Assorted stranded cottons (floss), flower threads, silks etc in floral colours – pinks, reds, greens

1 Using the Assisi Alphabet chart (pages 47–8), choose your initial.

2 Position the initial in the centre of the fabric and outline in back stitch using one strand of embroidery cotton (floss).

3 Using two strands of embroidery cotton (floss) over two threads of fabric, fill in the background in cross stitch leaving the Initial itself unworked (as in Assisi Initials). Use varying lengths of thread in a random fashion to create the effect of a flower-filled garden. (This enjoyable technique is much easier than it sounds.) Try also blending threads by threading your needle with two different colours, ie one strand of each.

Alternatives

1 Try working the design in alternative colours – eg, blues, lilacs and greys.

2 Work in wool on a larger-scale canvas to enlarge the design for a cushion.

3 Work over just one thread of linen to reduce the size of the design, for a brooch or pendant.

ROUND BIRTH SAMPLER

Delicately pretty, this charming pastel birth sampler (overleaf) would make a delightful gift. Cross stitch, back stitch, eyelet stitch, tent stitch and satin stitch are used – all with two strands over two threads of fabric except in the little birds which are filled-in with tent stitch over one thread. Refer to the key for colours.

Design size: 7½in (190mm) diameter

12 × 12in (305 × 305mm) white evenweave fabric, 25 threads per inch (25mm)
Stranded cottons (floss) as shown in the key

Begin by measuring 2½in (64mm) down from the top of your fabric and 5¼in (133mm) in from the left-hand side. Work the design from the chart as follows.

1st line Beginning with the ear of the rabbit on the left, work rabbits and dots in cross stitch. Outline the top left rabbit in 223 and the top right rabbit in 3755.

2nd line Work the hearts in cross stitch.

3rd line Work the houses in cross stitch.

4th line The small alphabet is worked in back stitch: letters d-j in 3755; k-o in 223; p-w in 955; x-c in 3042; d-j in 3755; k-o in 223; and p-t in 955.

5th line Work the flowerheads in eyelet stitch (each completed stitch covers four threads) beginning with 223 and alternating with 3755. Work the stems in back stitch in 955.

6th line Work the hearts in satin stitch beginning with ecru and alternating with 818.

7th line Outline the birds in back stitch: 1st bird 807; 2nd bird 3042; 3rd bird 3755; 4th bird 223. Repeat colour sequence for remaining birds. Fill-in the birds with tent stitch over just one thread, beginning with 818 and alternating with ecru.

8th line Work flowerheads in satin stitch beginning with 818 and alternating with 3042. Work stems in back stitch in 955.

9th line Work first two rows in back stitch in 3755 and third row in ecru. Work small eyelets over just one thread in 3755.

contd. on page 75

ROUND BIRTH SAMPLER

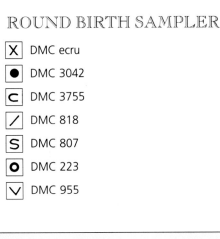

X	DMC ecru
●	DMC 3042
C	DMC 3755
/	DMC 818
S	DMC 807
O	DMC 223
V	DMC 955

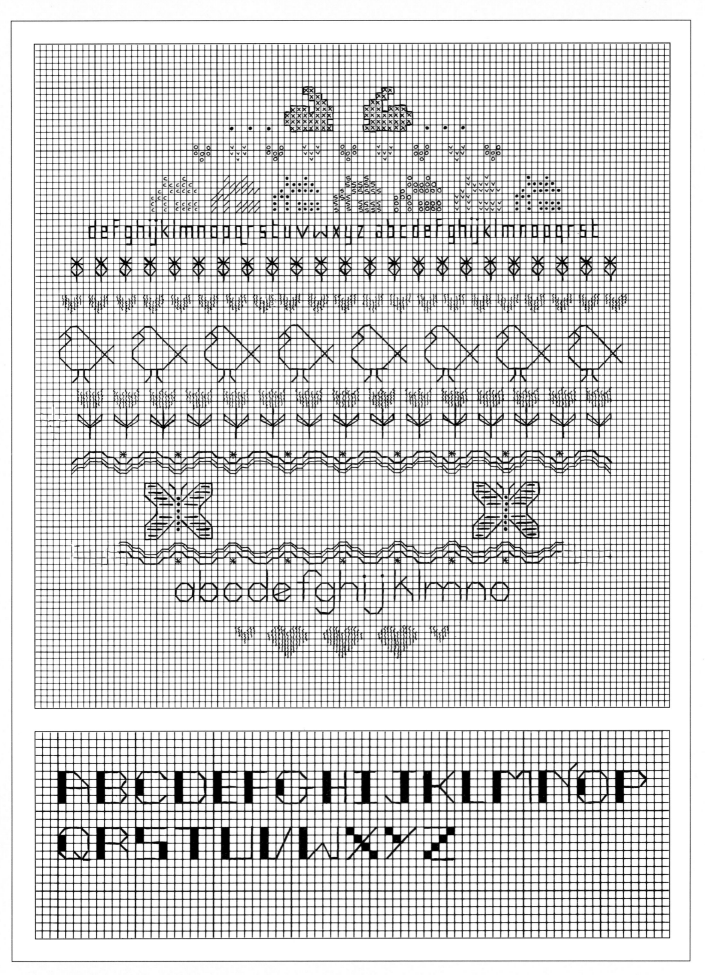

10th line Outline butterflies in back stitch in 807. The bodies are worked in cross stitch in 3042. Work satin stitch in-fill on the wings in 818. Work antennae in back stitch in 223. Chart your chosen name from the alphabet given, *in pencil*, using graph paper. Position as shown on the chart. If you choose a longer name, omit the butterflies.

11th line Reverse of 9th line.

12th line Work back stitch alphabet in 3042.

13th line Work hearts in satin stitch beginning with 955 and alternating with 223.

'ANNIE' CARD AND SMALL PICTURE

Elements of this design have been used to make a greetings card and small round picture (see photograph). Use the same fabric as for the sampler and the same range of colours, then follow these ideas – or create your own to suit your chosen name.

Round Birth Sampler, 'Annie'
Card and small picture

VICTORIAN HEART WITH INITIAL

*This romantic and fanciful Victorian-style
design, with ribbons, lace, flowers and birds worked in
delicate shades of blue, would look delightful
in a bedroom.*

Design size: 7 × 5¾in (178 × 145mm)
Stitch count: 95 × 80

10 × 11in (250 × 280mm) cream evenweave
  linen, 28 threads per inch (25mm)
DMC stranded cotton (floss) in shades of blue
  as shown in the key
Approximately 6in (150mm) very narrow blue
  ribbon
9 × 10in (230 × 255mm) cotton fabric for
  backing
1yd (1m) of 1in (25mm) cream lace
Piece of strong card
Tracing paper
Glue/impact adhesive

1 Centre the design on the fabric and work
in cross stitch following the chart, using
two strands of embroidery cotton (floss)
over two threads of linen.

2 Work the chosen initial from the alphabet
chart, positioning it as shown on the
chart.

3 When the embroidery is complete, make
a small bow from the ribbon, position it
on the heart as indicated on the chart
and attach using small stab stitches (use
one thread of matching cotton).

4 Using tracing paper, trace the heart given
on this page and cut round it to make a
template. Use this template to make a
heart in strong card.

5 Lay the embroidery face down on a clean
cloth and position the card on the back.
Fold the embroidered fabric over the
heart shape, ensuring that the card is
positioned evenly (to do this, insert
straight pins into the card's edge to hold
the fabric). Keep turning the design over
to check that it is in the right position
while you insert the pins. When you are
happy with the positioning, trim the
fabric to within 1⅛in (40mm) of the
card heart.

6 Make diagonal cuts in the folded-over
fabric to ease in the excess, then glue in
position using the impact adhesive.

7 When the glue is dry, cut a piece of
cotton fabric slightly larger than the
heart-shaped card. Place this fabric on
the back of the design and pin in place,
turning in the edges and trimming
where necessary. Hem stitch all around
the edge.

8 Pin the lace around the edge of the
design with the straight edge outwards
(frilly edge inwards), slightly gathering
and easing into place as you go.
Overstitch the lace to the edge. The
design is now ready for framing. A ready-
made heart-shaped frame has been used

in this case but you could ask your picture framer to make a heart-shaped mount which could then be used in a square frame.

Alternatives

1 This design would look very pretty as a cushion, perhaps centred into a square; use a larger piece of Quaker cloth and add a lace frill.

2 Reduce to half size by working over one thread of linen, to make a pincushion or appliqué motif for a child's dress.

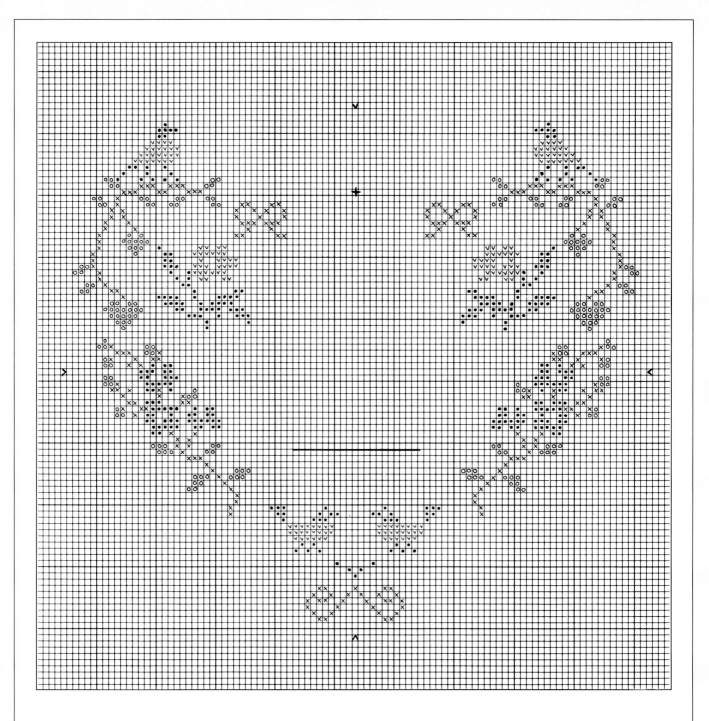

VICTORIAN HEART WITH INITIAL

Heart

● DMC 926

∨ DMC 598

X DMC 597

◉ DMC 927

Initial Alphabet

● DMC 598

X DMC 926

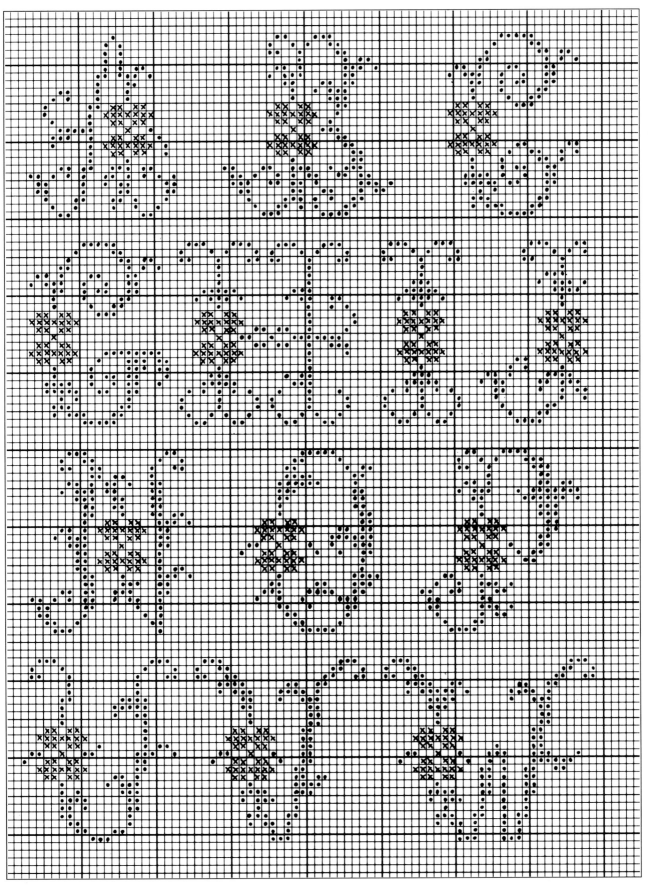

VICTORIAN ALPHABET

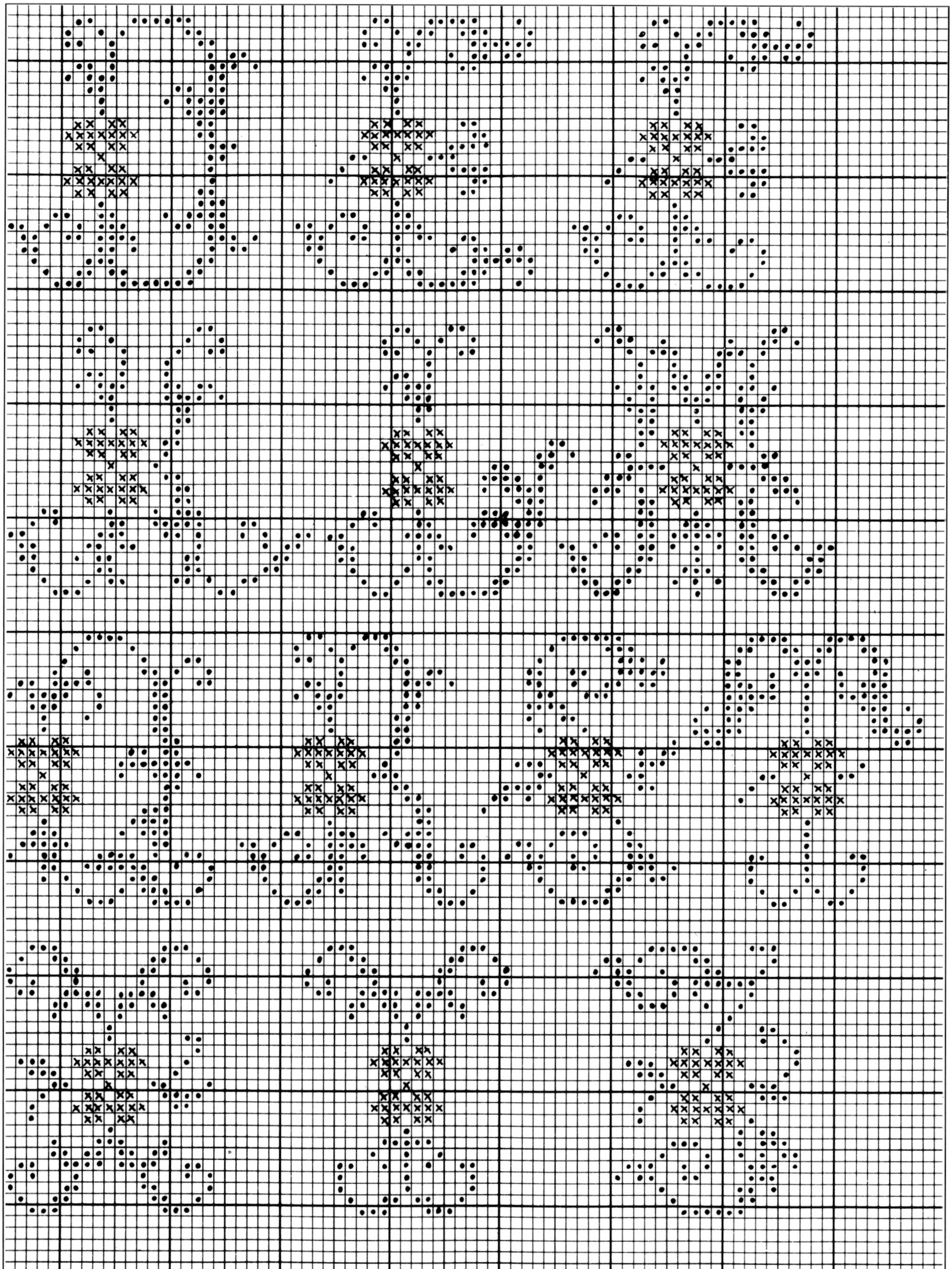

LONG STITCH INITIAL WITH ROSE BUSH

The combination (see overleaf) of painted canvas, a long stitch initial, ribbon roses and a fabric-covered mount, all in soft subtle colours, make this easy-to-work project very effective.

The design size varies, depending on the initial chosen.

8 × 8in (205 × 205mm) single-thread 14-count
  canvas
Stencil paint: Williamsburg blue
Stencil brush
DMC soft cottons (floss): 2495 (rose bush),
  2223 (initial)
6 small ribbon roses
8 × 8in (205 × 205mm) piece of strong card
9 × 9in (230 × 230mm) piece of small-print
  fabric for covering the card (the one shown
  is from Laura Ashley)
6½ × 6½in (165 × 165mm) card for mounting
The frame used is pine with a 'dragged paint'
  finish
Glue/impact adhesive

1 Begin by placing your piece of canvas on some sheets of newspaper. Using the stencil brush, apply the stencil paint evenly to the canvas. Leave to dry.

2 Measure 6in (153mm) down from the top of the canvas and 2½in (65mm) in from the right. At this point, begin working the base of the rose bush in long stitch, using one strand of soft cotton (floss) 2495.

3 Choose your initial from the Quilted Florentine Alphabet on page 33, position as shown on the chart and work in long stitch in soft cotton 2223.

Long Stitch Initial with Rose Bush

4 Position the ribbon roses where shown on the chart and attach to the work using small stab stitches in a matching thread.

5 Cut an aperture 5½ × 5½in (140 × 140mm) in the piece of strong card and cover with your chosen fabric.

6 After lacing your work to a piece of card 6½ × 6½in (165 × 165mm) position the covered card mount carefully on top and glue together (alternatively you could attach the two together with masking tape). The work is now ready for framing.

SEA-BACKGROUND INITIALS

'A life on the ocean wave' is brought to mind with this canvaswork design. The initial itself is worked in cross stitch in a very subtle variegated mohair-and-wool thread and the background is worked in perlé cotton.

Design size: 4½ × 4½in (115 × 115mm)

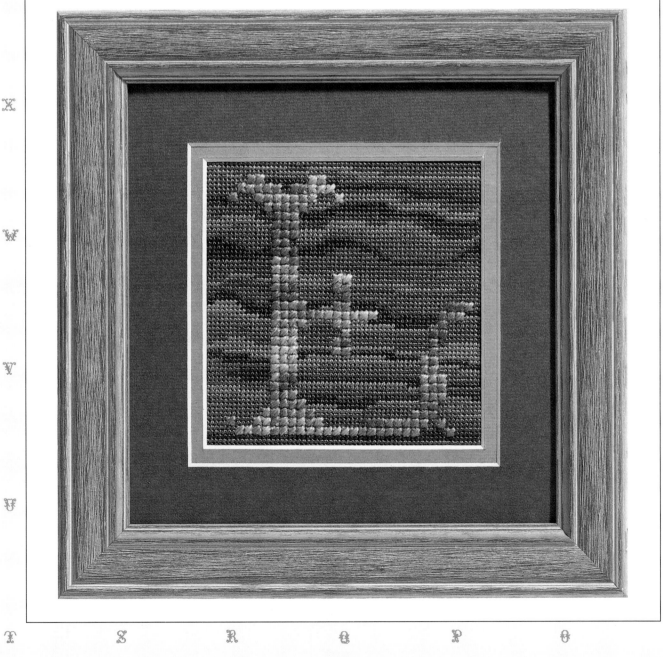

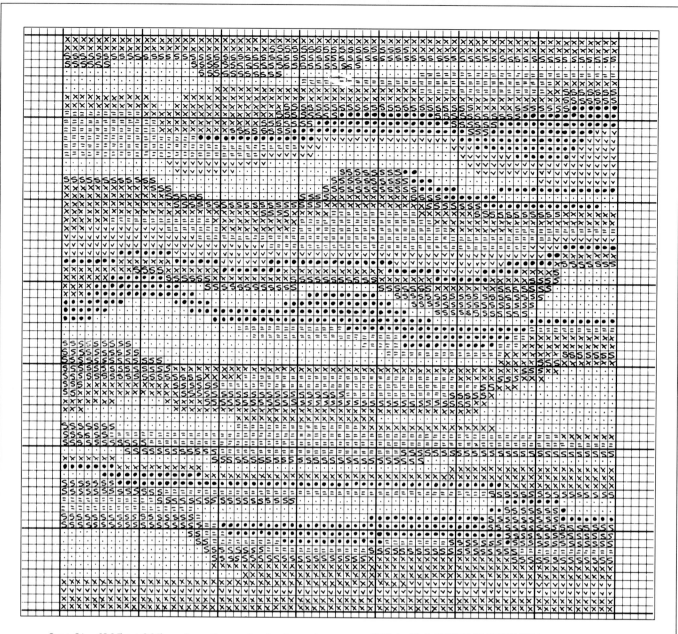

8 × 8in (205 × 205mm) antique single-thread
   14-count canvas
Variegated woollen thread from Brethyn Brith
   (or DMC variegated stranded cotton
   [floss]105) in beige/brown
Perlé cotton as shown in the key for the
   background
Tacking cotton (for outlining initial)

SEA-BACKGROUND

=	DMC 793	S	DMC 317
V	DMC 501	•	DMC 926
●	DMC 924	X	DMC 500

1 Using the Assisi Alphabet chart on pages
47–8, choose your initial.

2 Position the initial in the centre of the
canvas and outline in tacking cotton.

3 Using one strand of variegated thread (if
using Brethyn Brith) or three strands of

stranded cotton (floss) over two of
canvas, fill-in the initial in cross stitch.

4 Referring to the chart, fill-in the
background in tent stitch using one
strand of perlé cotton over one thread of
canvas. (One square on the chart
represents one tent stitch.)

INITIAL IN EYELET STITCH

This initial (overleaf) is taken from the French Alphabet shown on pages 94–5. The combination of space-dyed threads in silk on a richly coloured background, together with an unusual mount, make this initial look totally different. This design is worked entirely in eyelet stitch in Designer Silk over a four-block square of fabric, ie two blocks across and two down. Use one strand only of silk thread. (Designer Silk 703 contains more colours within this skein than you actually need, so be careful to choose only the grey/black colours for this design.) The main body of the letter and the leaves are worked in 703 grey/black. The flower is worked in 405 pink/mauve/purple.

Design size: 4½ × 5¼in (115 × 133mm)

8 × 9in (205 × 230mm) Charles Craft Wisteria 14-count Aida

1 Choose your initial from the French Alphabet chart.

2 Position your initial in the centre of the fabric.

3 Beginning at the middle point, work your initial in eyelet stitch as described above.

4 Lace your work onto strong card and position mount as shown, securing with double-sided tape.

Alternatives

1 Use an alternative colour scheme and frame with a simple mount.

2 Work in the colours given but in cross stitch over one block of fabric. This will considerably reduce the size of the work. Frame in a small round brass frame as shown, or use the small design as an appliqué motif.

INCA INITIAL

This colourful initial (overleaf) is created by using the Quilted Florentine Alphabet (page 34), in-filled with bright canvaswork repeats of Inca-inspired patterns. By choosing your own patterns from those given, you can create a piece that is totally unique. This design offers the opportunity to use up small pieces of leftover thread, and it is very enjoyable to work as every line is different.

Design size: 5⅝ × 3⅜ (143 × 85mm)

10 × 8in (255 × 205mm) antique 14-count
  mono canvas
DMC black crewel wool (Medici)
*An assortment of brightly coloured threads (as
  many as possible)*
Dark-brown ink (for dyeing the canvas)

1 Place the canvas on several sheets of newspaper and apply the dark-brown ink liberally and evenly. Leave to dry.

2 Choose your initial from the Quilted Florentine Alphabet chart. Using graph paper, enlarge the initial by treating each square on the chart as a block of four (for the outline only). Draw your enlarged initial lightly in pencil, altering its shape if appropriate. (In the example shown, the I has been fattened out slightly.) Work the outline in tent stitch using two strands of black crewel wool.

3 Choose patterns from the chart and, working in a variety of stitches, fill-in the outline of your initial. Patterns will not always finish evenly at the end of every line, but, as they are all small repeat patterns, this will not matter.

Alternatives

1 Try filling-in the outlined initials with different techniques – Rhodes stitch, cross stitch, satin stitch, etc.

2 Work on linen and fill-in the initial with blackwork patterns.

3 Work on linen, outline in white, then fill-in with whitework embroidery. The finished piece would make a wonderful centre square for a whitework cushion.

4 Try using the patterns on belts, cushions, bell pulls and guitar straps. (I have made several guitar straps for friends, using similar patterns and adding their initials repeated in a line to give continuity to the design.)

(opposite) Initial in Eyelet Stitch

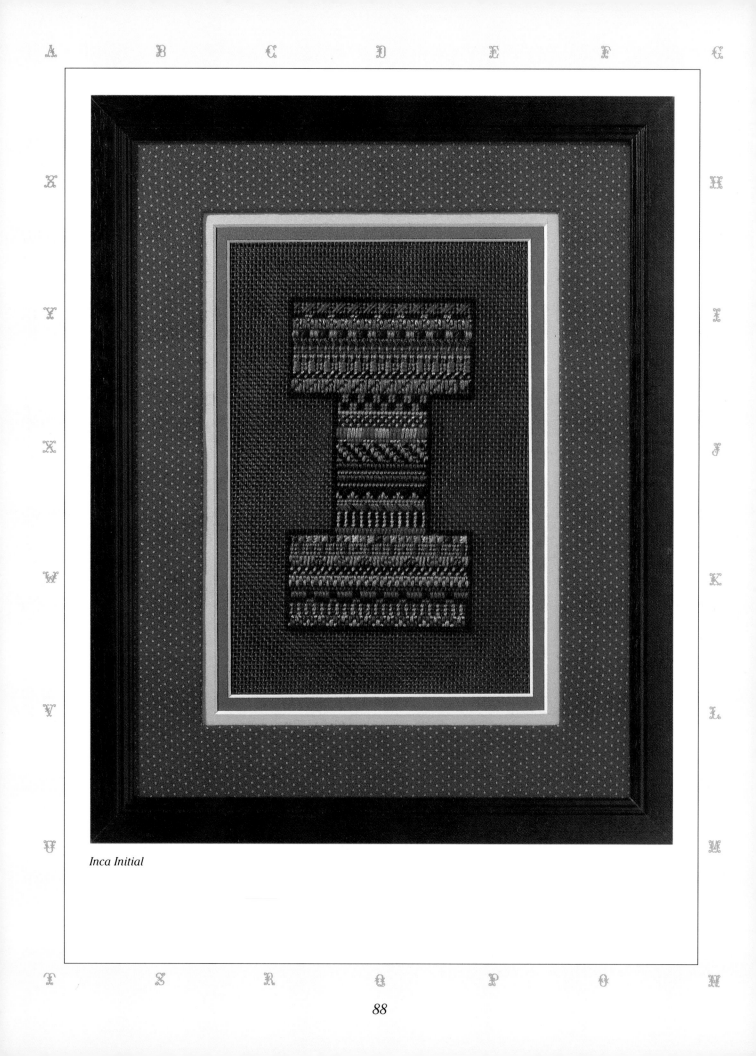

Inca Initial

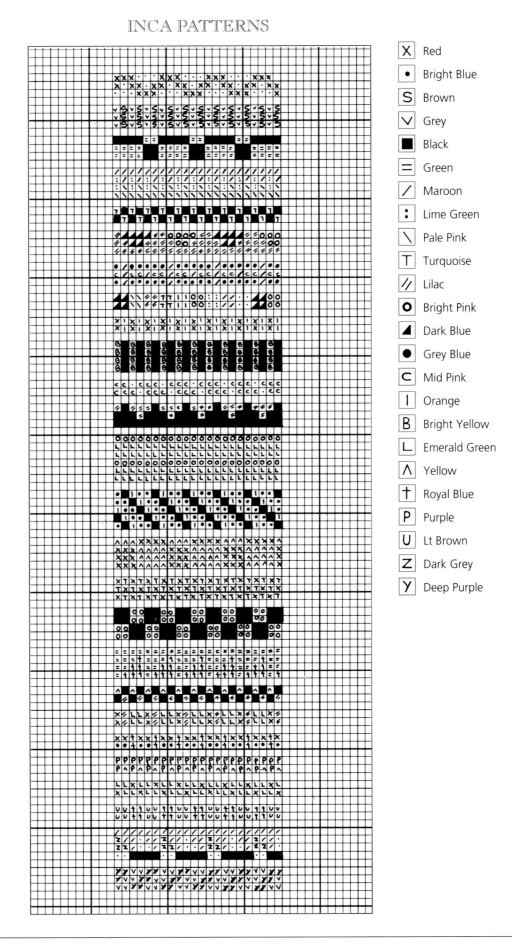

X	Red
•	Bright Blue
S	Brown
V	Grey
■	Black
=	Green
/	Maroon
:	Lime Green
\	Pale Pink
T	Turquoise
//	Lilac
O	Bright Pink
◢	Dark Blue
●	Grey Blue
C	Mid Pink
I	Orange
B	Bright Yellow
L	Emerald Green
∧	Yellow
†	Royal Blue
P	Purple
U	Lt Brown
Z	Dark Grey
Y	Deep Purple

VICTORIAN LACE INITIAL

This romantic design uses an initial from the French Alphabet (pages 94–5) on a ready-made jar lacy (jam-pot cover), mounted on a velvet-covered card. It is worked in cross stitch over one block of fabric using two strands of cotton (floss), in softer colours than those in the original French Alphabet.

One 2½in (63mm) round ivory jar lacy
DMC stranded cottons (floss): 368, 407, 758, 315, 890, 950 (see key on page 94)
Piece of strong card 9 × 9in (230 × 230mm)
Piece of plum-coloured cotton velvet 10 × 10in (255 × 255mm)
Cream-coloured sewing thread
Glue/impact adhesive

1 Choose your initial from the French Alphabet chart on pages 94–5.

2 Find the centre of the initial and match this to the centre of the jar lacy. Begin stitching at this point, following the Victorian Lace Initial colour key (in brackets) on the French Alphabet chart.

3 When the embroidery is complete, press lightly on the back of the design.

4 Position the embroidery in the centre of the velvet square (right sides uppermost) and tack together. Using small stab stitches and cream-coloured sewing thread, stitch the embroidered circle to the velvet.

5 Place the attached pieces face down and position the card 1in (25mm) from the edge all the way round. Mitre the corners of the fabric, apply glue to the edge of the card and to the wrong side of the fabric edges, then fold over the edges and press down firmly.

Alternatives

1 Make your own lace circle from a 3in (76mm) diameter piece of ivory 18-count Aida and 22in (560mm) of 1¾in (45mm) cream cotton lace. Oversew the circle, gathering the lace to fit, tack the lace to the circle's edge and either machine the edges together in a matching thread using zig-zag stitch, or use herringbone stitch.

2 The embroidered lace circle could be applied to the middle of a circular cushion (velvet or otherwise).

3 Attach the circle to a small hat-box lid, to make a very pretty box.

FRENCH ALPHABET

This elaborate alphabet with flowers and leaves twining round every letter can be used in many varied and exciting ways. It has been worked in tent stitch using two strands of cotton (floss) over just one thread of linen but if this causes eye strain, it can be worked over two threads (remember that this will double the size of the work).

Design size (worked over one thread):
5½ × 10in (140 × 255mm)
Stitch count: 152 × 280

10 × 14in (255 × 356mm) cream evenweave
  linen, 28 threads per inch (25mm)
DMC stranded cottons (floss) as shown in
  the key

Find the centre of the design, match it to the centre of the fabric and work from this point outwards, following the chart. It is advisable to use a frame to work this design, as tent stitch tends to distort the fabric, and enlarging the chart on a photocopier will make it easier to follow.

French Alphabet, Framed French
Initial and photograph frame

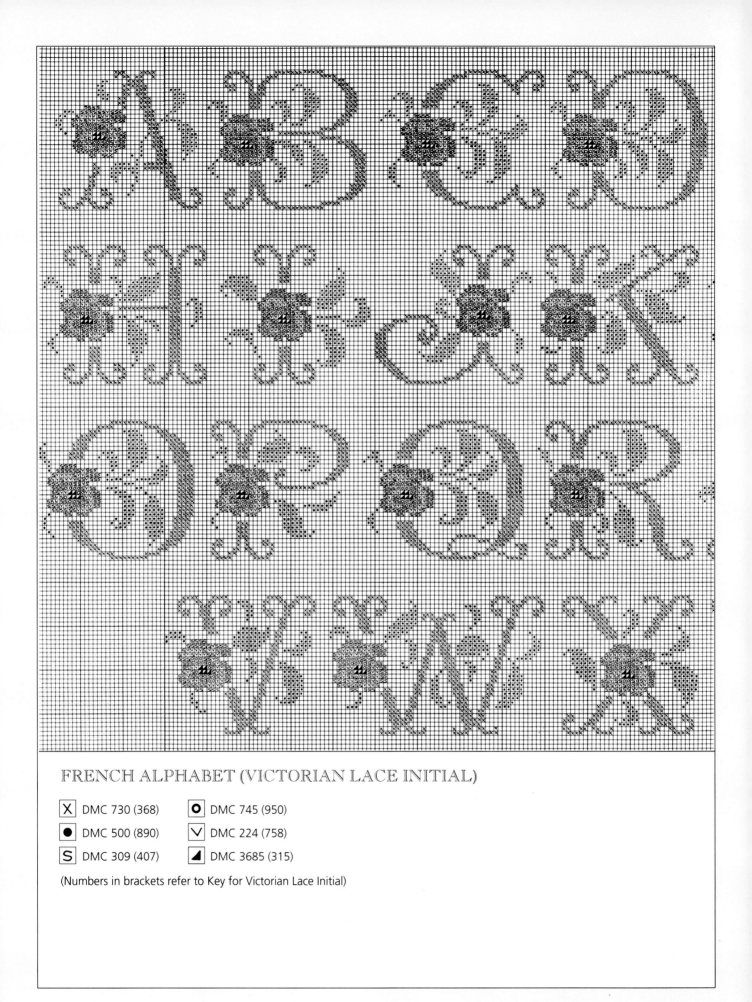

FRENCH ALPHABET (VICTORIAN LACE INITIAL)

X	DMC 730 (368)	O	DMC 745 (950)
●	DMC 500 (890)	V	DMC 224 (758)
S	DMC 309 (407)	◢	DMC 3685 (315)

(Numbers in brackets refer to Key for Victorian Lace Initial)

PHOTOGRAPH FRAME USING FRENCH ALPHABET INITIAL

Enhance a favourite photograph with this pretty, personalised mount, using an initial from the French Alphabet.

(No specific sizes are given for this project, as you will want to tailor the size to fit your own photograph)

White 22-count Hardanger fabric
Stranded cottons (floss) as shown in the Victorian Lace Initial key on the French Alphabet chart
Strong card
Glue/impact adhesive or masking tape

1 Measure your photograph to assess the size of aperture required. Allow sufficient fabric to enable you to work one (or maybe two) initial(s) of your choice, remembering also to allow for turnings to cover the card.

2 Mark the position of your aperture on the fabric with a border of tacking stitches.

3 Choose your initial from the French Alphabet chart. Position as shown on the photograph and work in cross stitch over one block of fabric using two strands of embroidery cotton.

4 Make up the embroidered fabric as a mount, position it carefully over your photograph and fix with masking tape or glue.

FRAMED FRENCH INITIAL

This initial R was worked on white evenweave fabric, 28 threads per inch (25mm). To enlarge the design, it was worked in cross stitch using two strands of embroidery cotton (floss) (colours as shown in the key for the French Alphabet) over two threads of fabric. Choose your initial from the French Alphabet chart.

BUTTON ALPHABET

In ice-cream colours on a cream background with added buttons, this nursery alphabet (overleaf) is deliciously different. Extremely quick and easy to make, it looks good as a complete alphabet, or partly worked as a name. It is worked in back stitch over two blocks of fabric, using three strands of cotton (floss) throughout.

Design size: 12½ × 9¼in (318 × 235mm)

17 × 14in (433 × 355mm) cream 14-count
  Aida fabric
DMC stranded cottons (floss): 3608, 743, 353,
  955, 3689
47 shirt buttons approx ⅜in (10mm) in the
  following colours:
  10 raspberry
  10 lemon
  10 pistachio
  9 peach
  8 strawberry

Find the centre of the design, match to the centre of the fabric and work from this point outwards, following the chart. Use the colours as shown in the photograph on page 99. Sew on the buttons back to front, ie with the flat side facing, as you work each letter, and finish securely.

Alternatives

1 Work a child's name and make up as a small cushion with a frill in toning colours. Attach a loop and use as a name cushion for the child's door.

2 Work a name on a sweater, following the knitwear rows as a grid.

3 Work button initials on a bookmark.

4 Work the child's name in the Button Alphabet and add further details such as the date, place of birth, weight, etc in a smaller alphabet (eg Christmas Alphabet chart on page 116). This would make a delightful birth sampler.

5 Work a child's name and frame with a hoop frill in toning colours.

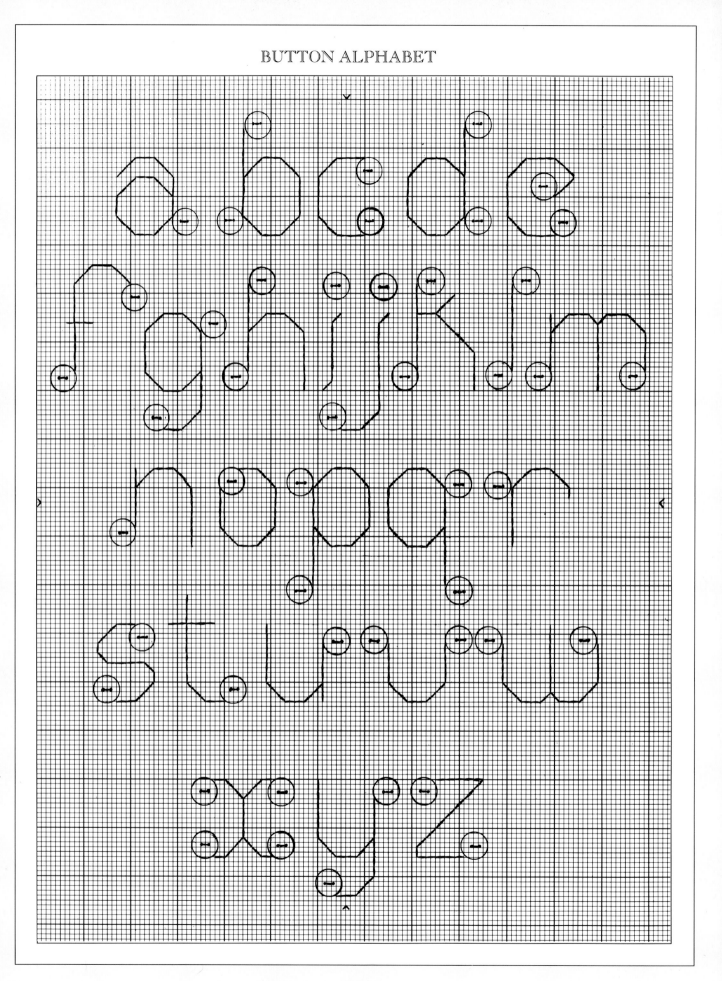

TRADITIONAL ALPHABET SAMPLER

This traditional cross stitch alphabet sampler (opposite) on 'antique' linen in soft subdued colours features four alphabets, numerals and pretty borders. It is worked in two strands of cotton (floss) over two threads of linen.

Design size: 17 × 11in (430 × 280mm)
Stitch count: 251 × 167

21 × 15in (535 × 380mm) unbleached
  Edinburgh linen, 36 threads per inch (25mm)
DMC stranded cottons (floss) as shown in
  the key

Find the centre of the design and work from this point outwards, following the chart.

TRADITIONAL ALPHABET INITIAL WITH BORDER

One of the large initials from the Traditional Alphabet sampler is here surrounded by a scaled-down version of the border to create a new design (see photograph on page 6). It is worked in cross stitch in two strands of cotton (floss) over two threads of linen.

Design size: 4¾ × 4¾in (120 × 120mm)
Stitch count: 83 × 83

7 × 7in (178 × 178mm) unbleached
  Edinburgh linen, 36 threads per inch
  (25mm)
DMC stranded cottons (floss) as shown in
  the key for the Traditional Alphabet
  Sampler

Find the centre of your chosen initial (from the Traditional Alphabet chart) and match to the centre of the chart shown on page 108. Mark the position of your initial lightly in pencil and match to the centre of the fabric. Begin work at this point and stitch, following the chart.

ABCDEFGHIJKLM
NOPQRSTUV
—— WXYZ ——

abcdefghijklmnopqrstuv
wxyz ××× 1234567890 ×××

ABCDEFG
HIJKLMN
OPQRSTU
VWXYZ
1234567890

abcdefghijklmnopq
rstuvwxyz —— 12345

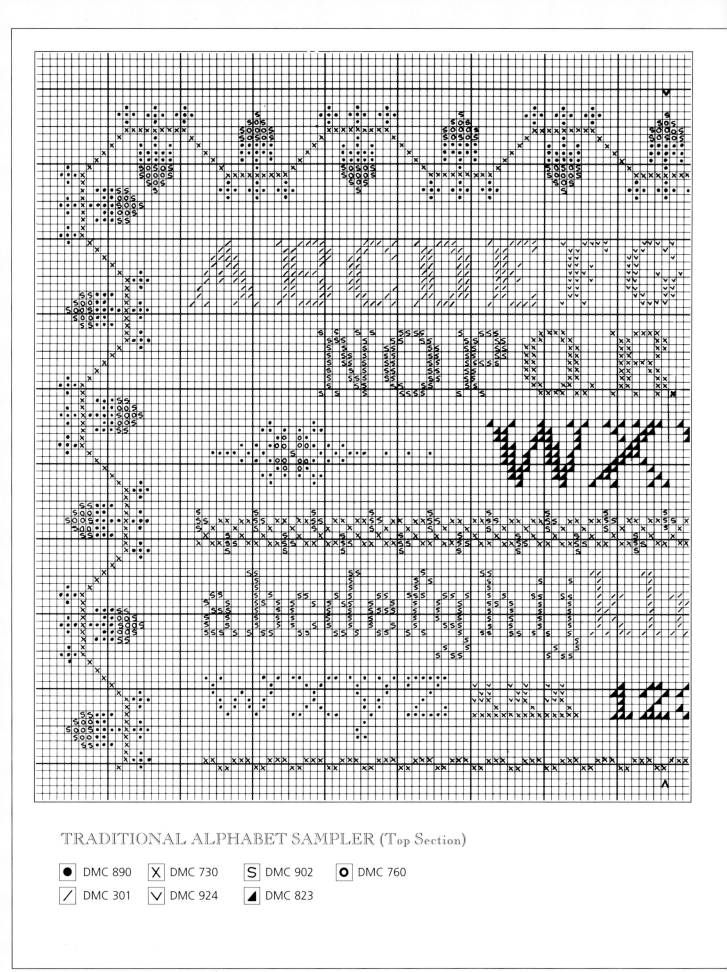

TRADITIONAL ALPHABET SAMPLER (Top Section)

● DMC 890	X DMC 730	S DMC 902	O DMC 760
/ DMC 301	V DMC 924	◢ DMC 823	

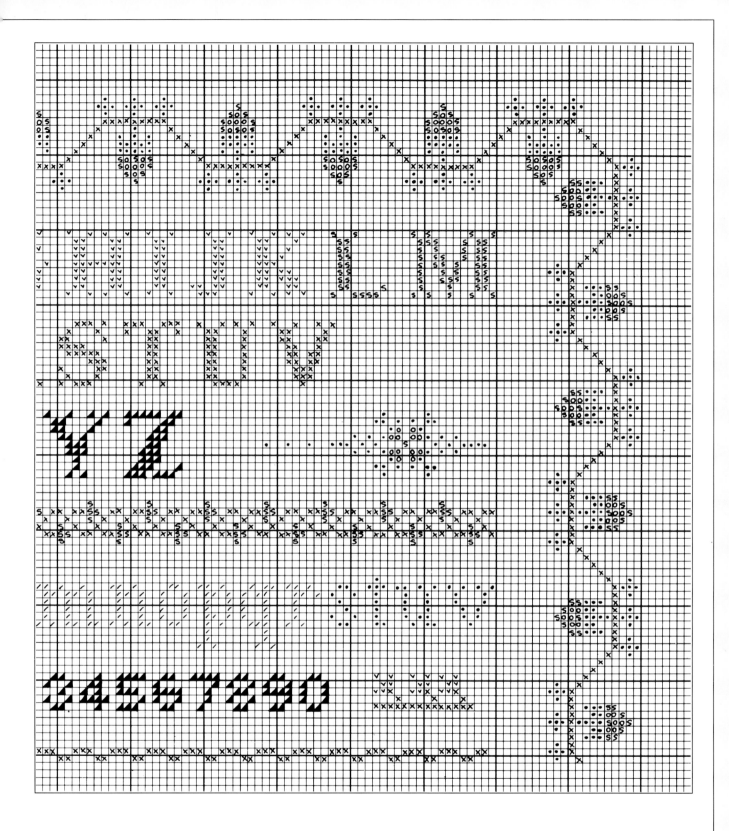

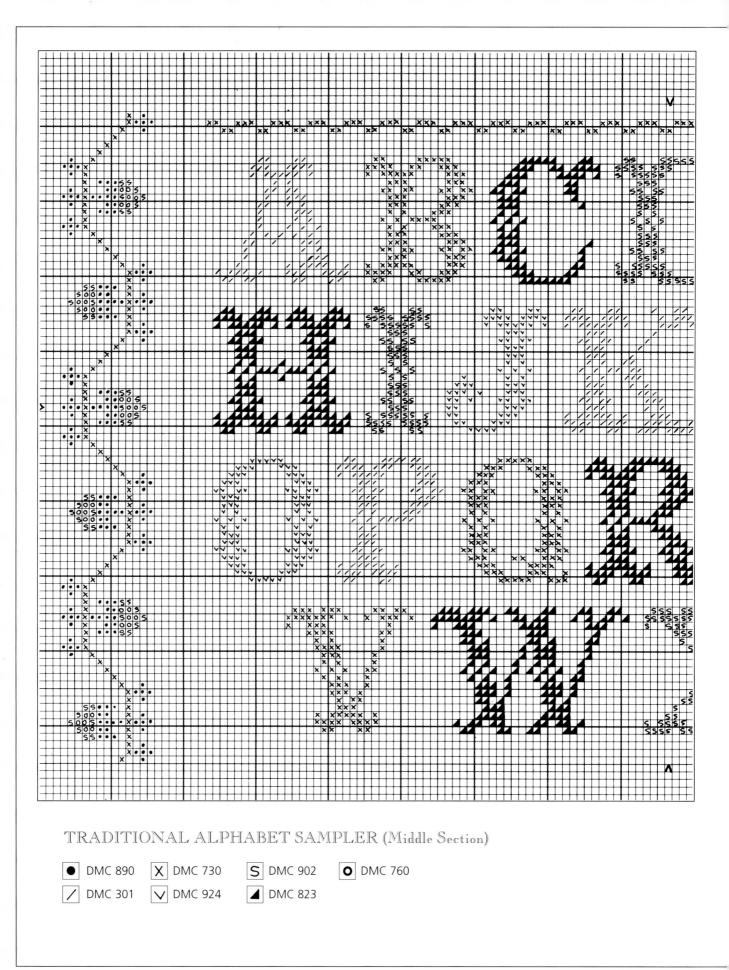

TRADITIONAL ALPHABET SAMPLER (Middle Section)

● DMC 890   X DMC 730   S DMC 902   O DMC 760

∕ DMC 301   V DMC 924   ◣ DMC 823

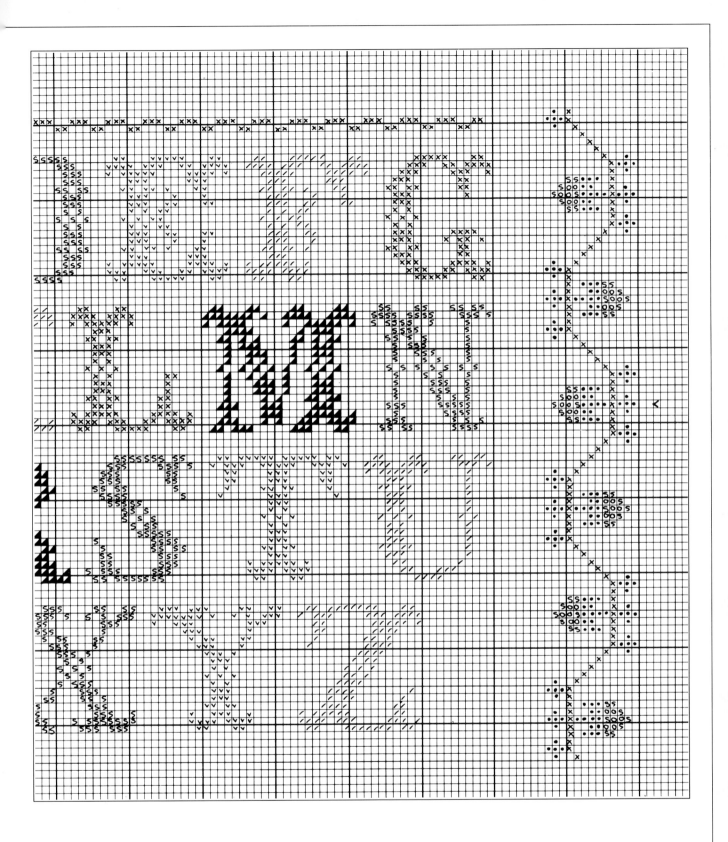

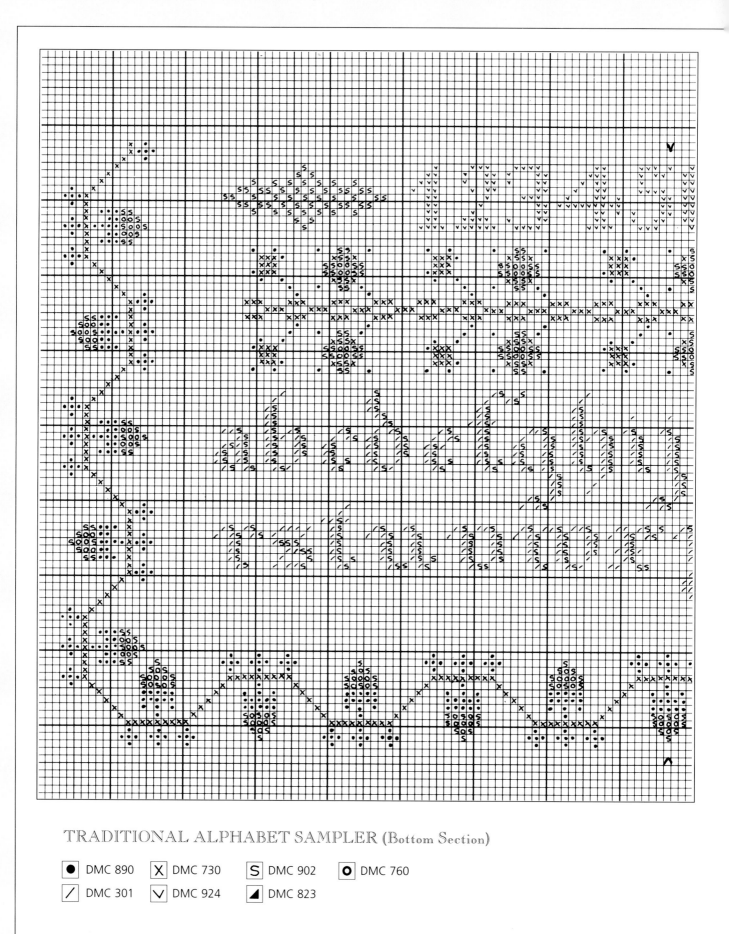

TRADITIONAL ALPHABET SAMPLER (Bottom Section)

● DMC 890   X DMC 730   S DMC 902   O DMC 760

/ DMC 301   V DMC 924   ◣ DMC 823

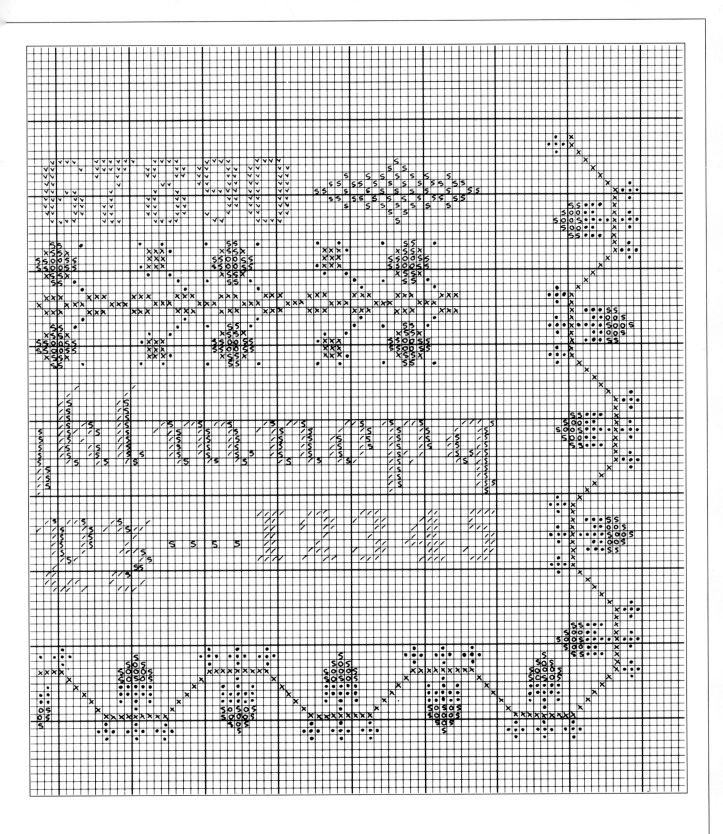

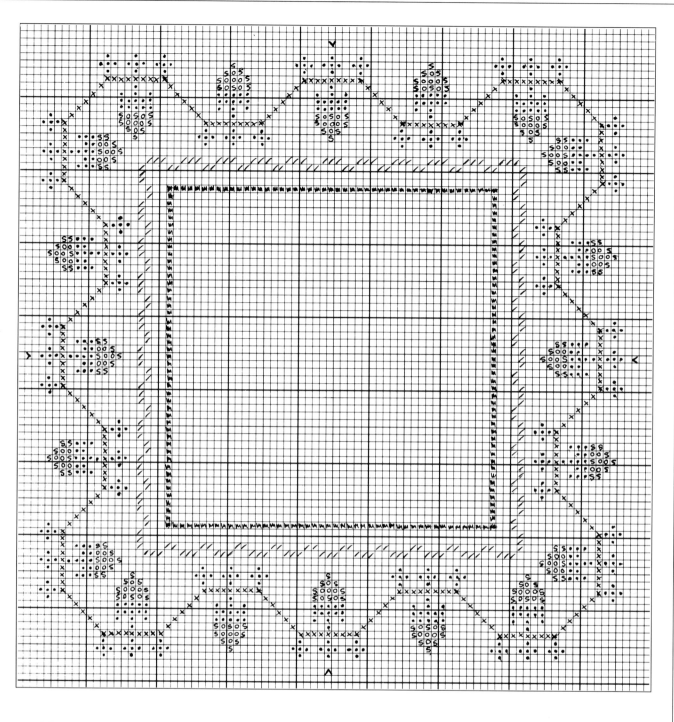

TRADITIONAL INITIAL WITH ALPHABET BORDER

- ● DMC 890
- X DMC 730
- S DMC 902
- O DMC 760
- / DMC 301
- V DMC 924
- W DMC 823

GOLDWORK INITIALS WITH A CHEQUERED BACKGROUND

Sophisticated and subtle, this initial (overleaf) is worked in reversed cushion stitch with a background of tent stitch squares. The border consists of five lines of diagonal satin stitch.

Design size: 3½ × 3½in (90 × 90mm)

7 × 7in (178 × 178mm) white 22-count petit-
point canvas
DMC stranded cottons (floss) as shown in
the key
DMC gold thread D282

1 Using the Goldwork Alphabet chart, choose your initial.

2 Find the mid-point of your initial and match this to the centre of the canvas.

3 Begin stitching at this point, working your initial in reversed cushion stitch in gold thread.

4 Fill-in the remaining background according to the chart, using two strands of embroidery cotton (floss) to work the multi-coloured squares in blocks of nine tent stitches.

5 Work the border in diagonal satin stitch over two threads of canvas.

BACKGROUND FOR GOLDWORK INITIALS

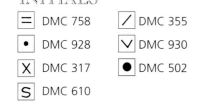

=	DMC 758	/	DMC 355
•	DMC 928	V	DMC 930
X	DMC 317	●	DMC 502
S	DMC 610		

Alternatives

1 Alternate every line in the border with gold thread.

2 Work the design entirely in wool on a larger mesh canvas, working the initial in Rhodes stitch to 'lift' and emphasise it.

3 Simplify the design by working the initials and background in cross stitch and the border in satin stitch.

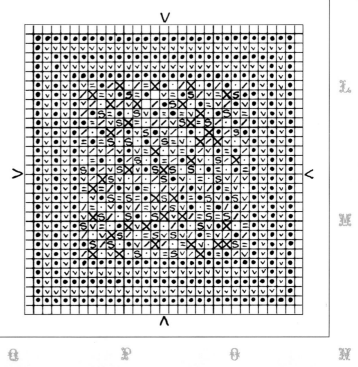

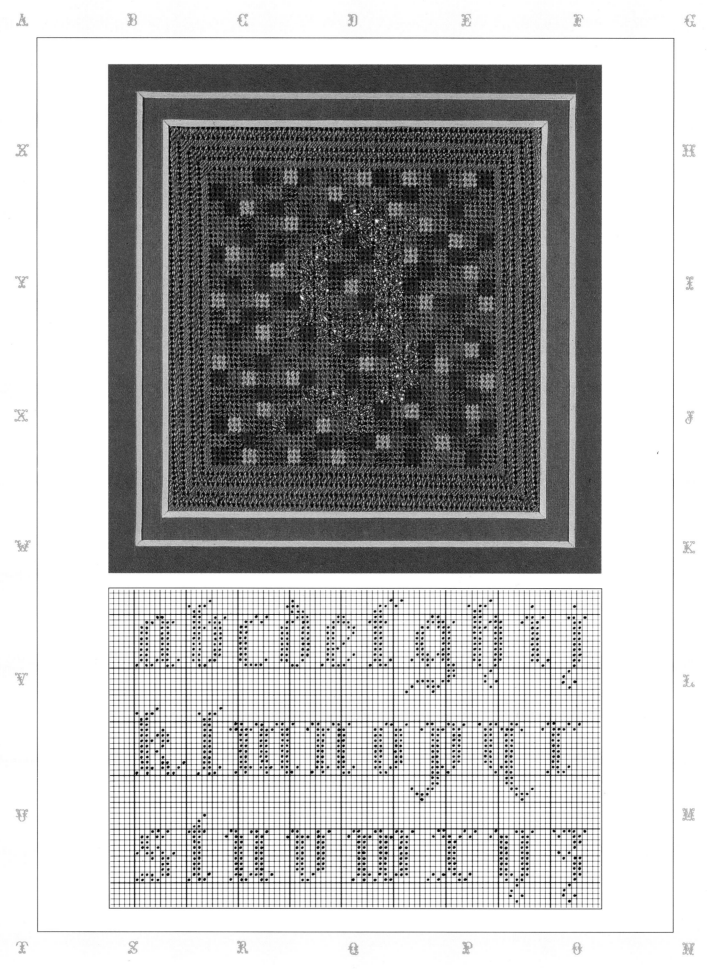

SCHOOLHOUSE
SAMPLER

This bold cross stitch alphabet sampler is strongly reminiscent of those worked by young girls in the nineteenth century. Use two threads of cotton (floss) over two threads of linen.

Design size: 10½ × 8in (265 × 205mm)
Stitch count: 133 × 101

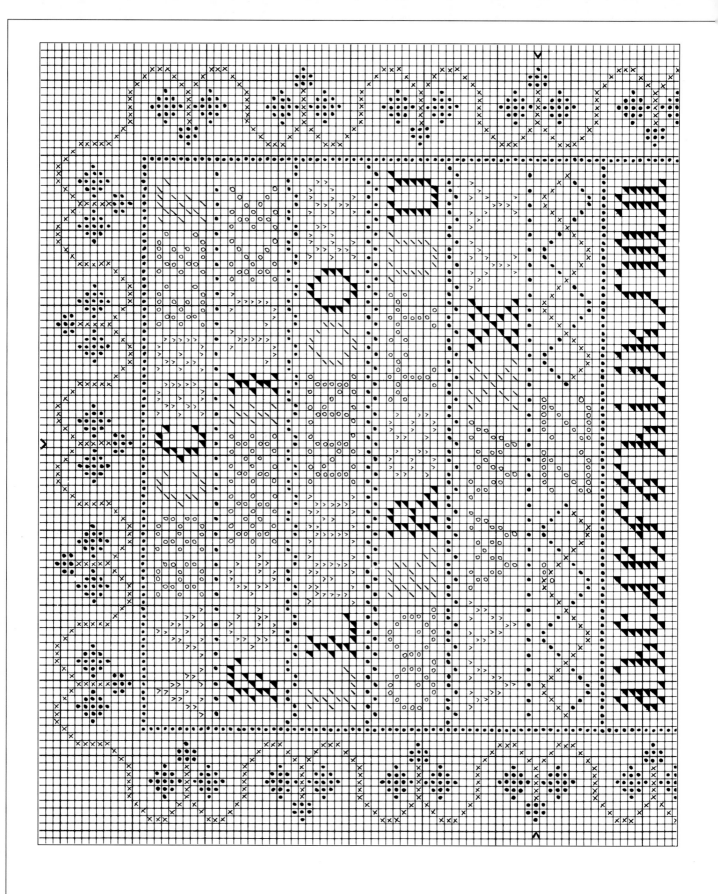

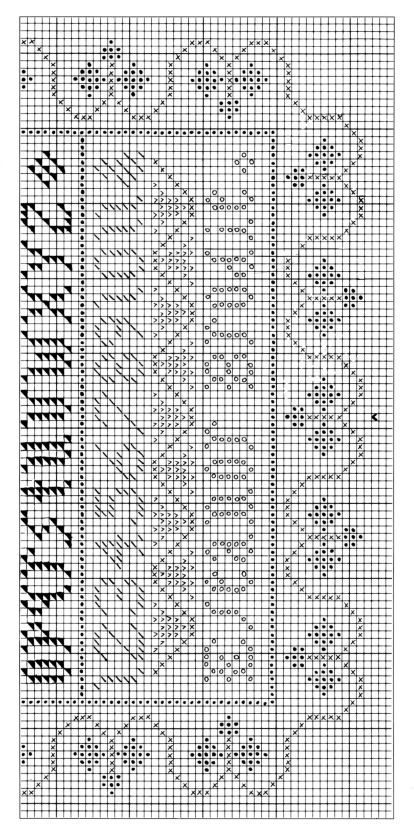

14 × 12in (355 × 306mm) natural evenweave linen, 25 threads per inch (25mm)
DMC stranded cottons (floss) as shown in the key
Purchased frame

Find the centre of the design, and work from this point outwards. If you wish to personalise this sampler, use the alphabets given within it to chart your own name, on graph paper. Position as shown on the chart. If you have a long name or wish to include the date, substitute initials for your christian name(s).

SCHOOLHOUSE SAMPLER

| ● | DMC 902 | X | DMC 732 | V | DMC 300 |
| O | DMC 347 | / | DMC 501 | ◢ | DMC 823 |

CHRISTMAS ALPHABET PROJECTS

A very simple lower case Christmas Alphabet has been used for these colourful projects: the Noel banner, Christmas card, tree decorations and trinket pot lids. They are a good example of the effectiveness of repeated names or words.

NOEL BANNER

12 × 6½in (305 × 165mm) white evenweave linen, 25 threads per inch (25mm)
DMC stranded variegated cottons (floss) 75 and 114
DMC gold thread D282
Set of 7½in (190mm) wooden hanger rods

1 Measure 2in (50mm) from the top of the fabric and 1¼in (32mm) in from the left. Begin stitching the word Noel in back stitch over two threads in DMC 75 using three strands. Repeat the word, leaving a space of eight threads between. Work to within 1¼in (32mm) of the right side. Begin the next line by staggering the words as shown and leaving a space of six threads between the main body of the lettering. Work five lines in this way.

2 Change to DMC 114 and work as indicated above for five lines.

3 Change to DMC gold thread D282 (do not separate strands) and continue as above for another six lines.

Noel Banner, Tree Ornaments, Trinket Pots and Card

4 When the embroidery is complete, make a ¼in (6mm) hem on the long sides of the embroidered piece. For added effect, you may like to withdraw two threads next to the line of hemming, to give an interesting edge to the design.

5 Make a ½in (12mm) hem at the top and bottom of the piece, leaving the ends open so that the wooden rods can be passed through. Fit the wooden rods.

TREE ORNAMENTS

Small pieces of white evenweave (or coloured) linen
DMC stranded cottons (floss) in your own choice of colours
Purchased tree ornament frames

Work your chosen lettering from the Christmas Alphabet (as for the Noel Banner) and fit into the frames, following the manufacturer's instructions. The more colourful you make these ornaments, the better. Try using up small pieces of left-over thread instead of using manufacturer's variegated thread. Work until your length of thread runs out and re-start with a different colour. This will give a wonderfully bright and varied effect.

TRINKET POTS

Evenweave linen, 25 threads per inch (25mm) or 14-count Aida (in colours to match the pot of your choice)

DMC stranded cottons (floss) in your own choice of colours
Purchased trinket pots

1 Using the size of the trinket pot lid as a guide, cut a piece of your chosen fabric at least 1in (25mm) bigger all the way round.

2 Work your chosen lettering from the Christmas Alphabet, following the instructions given for the Noel Banner.

3 When your embroidery is complete, fit it into the trinket pot lid following the manufacturer's instructions.

'TIS THE SEASON TO BE JOLLY CARD

White evenweave linen, 28 threads per inch (25mm)
DMC stranded cottons (floss) in your own choice of colours
Glissengloss (specialised thread resembling tinsel)
Purchased card (or make your own)
Glue

Work your chosen lettering from the Christmas Alphabet, following the instructions given for the Noel Banner. Fit your embroidery into the card. Apply a small amount of glue to the edge of the aperture and, when tacky, press glissengloss thread into place.

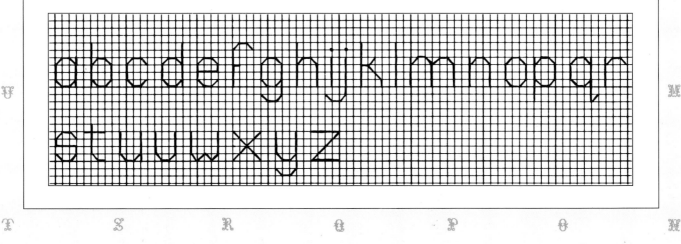

BEADED NOEL PROJECTS

These very quick and easy-to-make projects (see pages 118–19) are bright and festive, with their gold threads and beads. The card can be used as a decoration in its own right.

BEADED NOEL HOOP

Design size: (of word) 1 × 5¼in (25 × 135mm)
Stitch count: 13 × 70

10 × 10in (250 × 250mm) red 14-count Aida fabric
DMC stranded cotton (floss) 500
DMC gold thread D282
Madeira Glamour thread dark green 2458
4 small gold-coloured beads
8in (205mm) wooden embroidery hoop
For the hoop frill:
54 × 7in (1,372 × 178mm) Christmas cotton print
21in (535mm) of 2in (50mm) tartan ribbon
Small piece of artificial holly
Small piece of ribbon or tape

1 Begin by positioning the fabric evenly in the hoop.

2 Measure 4½in (115mm) from the top of the hoop and work a line of tacking stitches to show the base line for the word.

3 Measure 1½in (38mm) in from the left side of the hoop on the base line and begin stitching the base of the letter N in cross stitch, following the chart, using two strands of embroidery cotton (floss) DMC 500 over one block of fabric.

4 When the cross stitch is complete, work straight irregular stitches in the DMC gold thread as shown, to simulate tinsel.

5 Using two strands of Madeira Glamour thread, work long stitches (to 'hang' the beads) as shown on the chart.

6 Attach the gold-coloured beads, using a toning thread, in the position shown on the chart.

7 When the embroidery is complete, trim the fabric in the hoop so that 1in (25mm) protrudes from the frame. Oversew this edge to prevent fraying.

8 Make the hoop frill and attach.

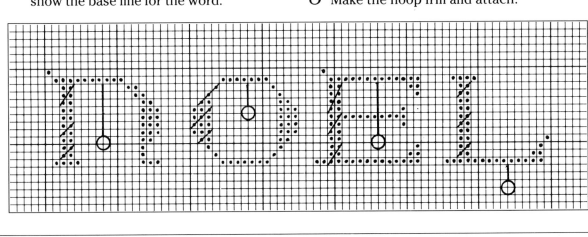

9 Make a bow from the ribbon and stitch to the bottom middle of the hoop to cover the join in the hoop frill.

10 Using small stitches in a toning thread, stitch the artificial holly to the middle of the bow, securing well.

11 Finally, using a small piece of left-over ribbon make a loop to hang up the hoop and stitch to the back of the embroidery (where it protrudes from the hoop).

Beaded Noel Hoop, Banner and Card

BEADED NOEL BANNER

Design size (of word): 6½ × 1¾in
(165 × 45mm)
Stitch count: 61 × 16

9in (230mm) piece of white 'linen band', 30
threads per inch (25mm)
DMC stranded cotton (floss) red 817
Madeira Glamour dark green 2458
DMC gold thread D282
4 small gold-coloured beads
Pair of small brass bell-pull hangers

1 Measure 1¼in (32mm) from the
bottom of the linen band (this is the base
line for stitching). Match together the
mid-point of the bottom line of the 'L' and
the mid-point of the base line and begin
stitching here in cross stitch over three
threads of linen in DMC 817. Work the
'tinsel' in irregular straight stitches in
Madeira Glamour 2458 and the
thread for hanging the beads in DMC
gold D282. Attach the beads in position
as shown, using one strand of the
gold thread.

2 Make a ½in (12mm) hem at the top and
bottom of the linen band, iron on the
wrong side and insert the brass hangers
(they are split in the middle and are
therefore easy to insert).

BEADED NOEL CARD

Design size (of word): 4 × 1in (100 × 25mm)
Stitch count: 61 × 16

9in (230mm) piece purchased red 'linen band'
30 threads per inch (25mm)
Threads as for the Beaded Noel Hoop
4 small gold-coloured beads
Piece of stiff green paper or thin card 11 × 8¼in
(280 × 210mm)
Glue/impact adhesive

1 Measure 2½in (63mm) from the bottom of
the linen band (this is the base line for
stitching). Match together the mid-point
of the bottom line of the 'L' and the mid-
point of the base line and begin stitching
here, following the stitch instructions for
the Beaded Noel Hoop but stitching over
two threads of linen.

2 When the embroidery is complete, fray
¾in (19mm) at the bottom of the linen
band as shown.

3 Fold the piece of card in half across
the width.

4 Make a fold in the top of the linen
band ¾in (19mm) and press on the wrong
side. Spread a small amount of glue
to the underside of this fold. Fold this
glued edge over the top of the front
page of the folded card in the middle
as shown.

STITCH DIRECTORY

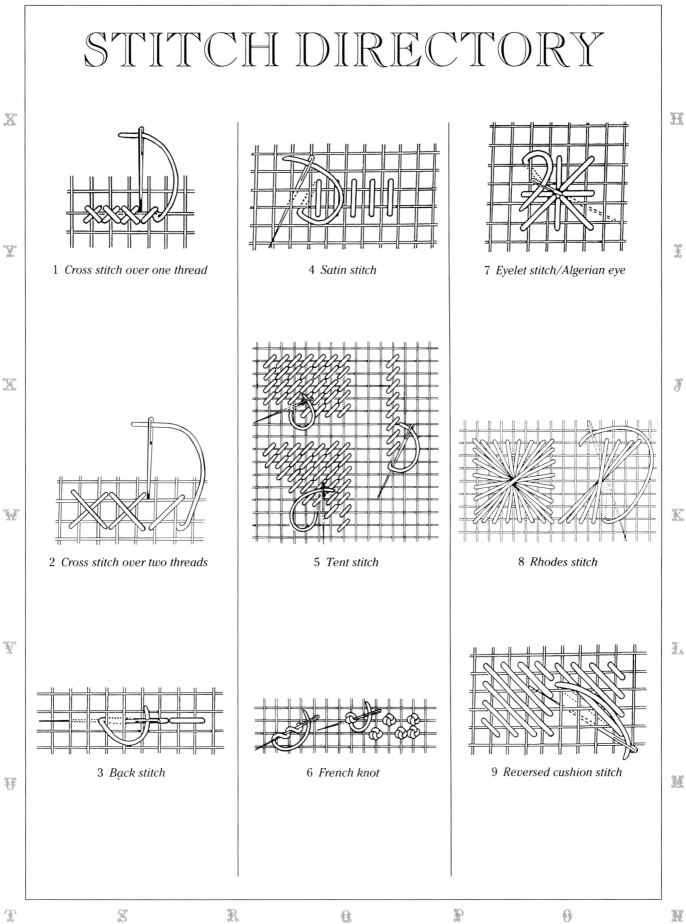

1 *Cross stitch over one thread*

4 *Satin stitch*

7 *Eyelet stitch/Algerian eye*

2 *Cross stitch over two threads*

5 *Tent stitch*

8 *Rhodes stitch*

3 *Back stitch*

6 *French knot*

9 *Reversed cushion stitch*

FINISHING, MOUNTING AND FURTHER TECHNIQUES

When your embroidery is complete, there are a number of things to do before taking it to the framers or framing it yourself.

1 First check your design against the chart. It is so easy to leave out stitches or even whole areas of the design, which may be missed in the euphoria that follows the completion of your work.

2 Turn the work over, check that all loose ends are secure, then snip off any trailing threads. (Trailing dark threads especially will show through and ruin the appearance of the finished work.)

3 If at all possible, avoid washing and ironing your work. If you have taken steps to protect it while in progress, and have used an embroidery frame or hoop large enough to encompass not only the work but also a reasonable margin for framing, then washing and ironing should not be necessary. If, for some reason, it is necessary, wash by hand, taking great care not to rub or wring. Use lukewarm water with mild soap flakes and gently swish the work about. Rinse well then roll in a clean white towel. Open out and leave to dry. If you have washed your work, then it will be necessary to press it. To do this, lay a clean, dry, white towel on an ironing board. Lay the work face down on the towel and press

lightly. This method will prevent the stitches being flattened.

Mounting your work

It is *always* worth going to the trouble of mounting your work properly. Otherwise, it will pucker and crease.

1 Cut a strong piece of acid-free mount board (available from good art shops) or hardboard (covered with acid-free paper), either slightly bigger than your embroidery if a mount is to be used or, if not, to the size of your chosen frame.

2 Place the card or covered hardboard on the wrong side of the embroidery. When in position, secure with straight pins inserted into the edge, frequently turning and checking that the embroidery is placed correctly.

3 Fold over the side edges of the fabric, then use a long length of strong thread to lace back and forth (a). Pull up the stitches to tighten and secure firmly.

4 Complete the top and bottom in the same way (b).

Fabric-covered mounts

Fabric-covered mounts allow the use of a great variety of colour schemes – plain and patterned. You will need: strong card, fabric, glue/impact adhesive, a metal rule, a scalpel or craft knife, and a cutting board or several layers of card to protect the surface you are cutting on.

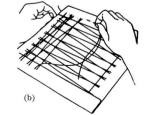

(a)   (b)

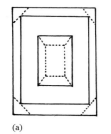

(a)   (b)

Covering a mount with fabric

1 Measure the completed embroidery carefully and cut the card mount and the aperture to the size required.

2 Cut the fabric to the size of the mount *plus* allowances for turnings (this allowance will vary according to the size of the mount and the type of covering fabric – for instance, velvet requires a larger allowance than cotton). Make sure that you align the mount with the straight grain of the fabric.

3 Place the fabric right side down and position the mount in the middle. Snip off the corners of the fabric as shown by the dotted lines in (a).

4 Apply the adhesive to the remaining fabric at the outer edge. Fold over and press flat.

5 To cut out the inside 'window', first cut out the rectangle as shown by the dotted line and then carefully snip into the corners stopping just short of the edge. Apply adhesive to this remaining fabric, fold over and press flat (b).

6 Carefully align the mount over the embroidery and fix with glue or masking tape.

Framing

The choice of frame plays an important part in the success of the finished piece. The frame and/or mount must complement the embroidery and not merely house it. A relatively simple piece of work can be transformed if careful thought is given to the choice of frame and/or mount.

This need not mean a great deal of expense. Simple wooden picture frames can be improved by painting them. Sample-size pots of paint are ideal for this purpose. The picture frame on page 82 was finished using two of these pots. A coat of pale pink was applied first, then, before this was dry, pale-blue paint was applied at random and 'dragged' across the surface with a clean lint-free cloth. When the paint was completely dry, a coat of matt varnish was applied.

Here are some other ideas to brighten up plain frames:

1 Paint frames with gloss to match your embroidery and/or your decor (sand down and undercoat first).

2 Paint the frame in one colour, then, dip an old toothbrush in a contrasting colour and flick the paint onto the frame, to give a stippled effect.

3 To give a limed effect to a wooden frame, first paint in your chosen colour. When dry, rub a little ready-mixed Polyfilla into the grain and corner joins, wiping off the excess. When this is dry, finish with a coat of matt varnish.

4 Re-vamp old frames by sanding and, either, painting as suggested or varnishing (traditional or coloured varnish).

5 To make a padded frame, cut a card mount with the appropriate size aperture, and three layers of terylene wadding to same size and shape as the mount with the aperture. Follow the instructions given for fabric-covered mounts, adding the wadding between the fabric and card.

When framing, you will have to decide whether to use non-reflective glass, plain glass or no glass at all. Unless your work has a very raised textured appearance, the use of glass is advisable to protect from dust and dirt. Plain glass is preferable. Non-reflective sounds a good idea but in practice it tends to give the work a slightly mottled and flat appearance. Whichever glass you choose, make sure that it does not come into contact with the needlework. If you are not using a mount, ask your picture framer to use thin strips of card to prevent contact between the work and the glass.

Making a Fold-Over Card

You may not want to go to the trouble of making your own card and, indeed, there are many excellent ready-made varieties available (see Suppliers). If, however, the size or colour you want is not available, then the following instructions will enable you to tailor your card to your own requirements.

1 Choose thin card in a colour to match your design.

2 Measure your embroidery to assess the size and shape of the aperture. (Round, oval and heart-

A   B   C   D   E   F   G

X   H

Y   I

X   J

W   K

V   L

U   M

T   S   R   Q   P   O   N

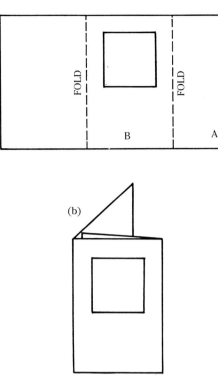

(a)

(b)

3 Make folds as shown in (a) opposite and press.

4 Tack the lace to the raw edge of the fabric (right side facing) and fold as shown in (b).

5 Fold again as shown in (c) and then pin, tack and machine or hand stitch through all layers close to the fold as shown in (d).

6 Unscrew the hoop and slot the outer part through the fabric frill as shown in (d). Replace the screw, but do not tighten fully. Ease onto the inner frame which has the embroidery positioned over it. Adjust the screw until the outer frame will just fit over the embroidery. Ease the frill, adjusting the gathers until they are evenly distributed. Make a small turning on one edge and oversew to the remaining edge. Finish the hoop with ribbon bows, silk or dried flowers etc, positioning them so that they hide the join of the frill. Attach with small stitches in a toning thread.

7 Make a small loop with ribbon for hanging and attach to the back of the fabric frill at the top with small stitches.

Charting Names and Dates

If you wish to personalise your work, for example by adding your name and the date to a sampler, this is relatively easy to do.

1 First check the amount of space available, by counting the number of squares on your chart.

2 Choose your alphabet, taking its size into consideration. If, for example, you would like to use a larger alphabet than would fit the space available width-wise, you could consider using your initials, surname and the date, or maybe just your initials and the date. Work out your details *in pencil* on graph paper, adjusting the spacing to suit the letters chosen. For example, a lower case i placed next to a lower case l usually looks better with two spaces between if the alphabet is very plain (even if only one space is allowed between the other letters). This type of adjustment will sometimes be necessary between other letters but this will quickly become apparent during the charting process.

3 When you have worked out your details, count the number of squares used vertically and horizontally and position the lettering evenly and centrally in the appropriate place on the embroidery.

shaped apertures can be particularly tricky to cut accurately unless you are skilled in this area.) Do not attempt to cut any aperture with scissors, always use a craft knife or scalpel.

3 Referring to (a), cut your card to the size and shape required. Cut an aperture in 'B' and with your craft knife lightly score fold lines as indicated by the dotted lines.

4 Position the aperture over your embroidery. Trim away any excess fabric and glue into position or secure with double-sided sticky tape.

5 Fold 'A' over 'B' and glue together (b). For a simple fold-over card in which the embroidery is attached to the front without a mount (as in the Noel card, page 116), cut a piece of card twice the size of the desired front area, measure and mark where the fold is required and score with a craft knife as above. Attach the embroidery with adhesive or double-sided sticky tape.

How to make a Gathered Hoop Frill

1 Cut your fabric 7in (178mm) wide × twice the circumference of the hoop plus 6in (153mm) (or more if you want a very full frill).

2 If you are adding lace, cut to the same length as the fabric.

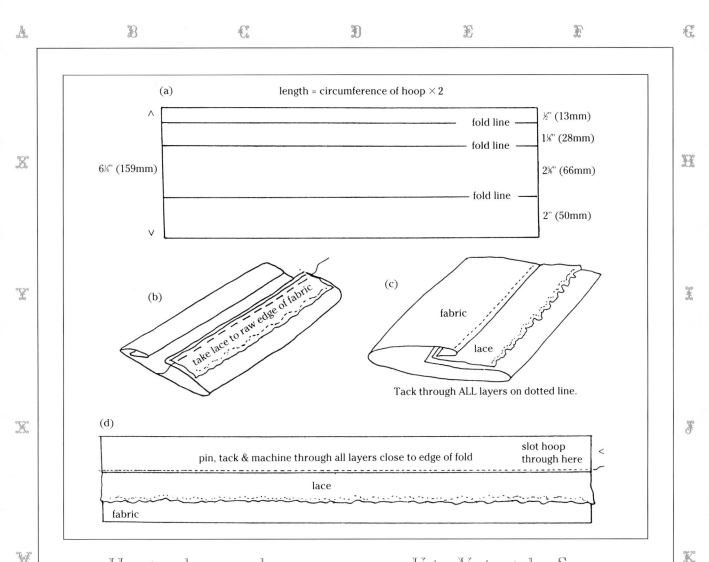

(a) length = circumference of hoop × 2

6¼" (159mm)

fold line — ½" (13mm)
fold line — 1⅛" (28mm)
2⅝" (66mm)
fold line —
2" (50mm)

(b) take lace to raw edge of fabric

(c) fabric

lace

Tack through ALL layers on dotted line.

(d)

pin, tack & machine through all layers close to edge of fold   slot hoop through here

lace

fabric

How to enlarge or reduce a Charted Design

The beauty of charted designs is the ease with which they can be enlarged or reduced. If, for example, you want to use a small but elaborate initial as a design for a cushion panel, you can increase its size in two ways: by considering every square in the design to be two, three or even four stitches square instead of one; and by increasing the number of threads or blocks of fabric worked over. For example, if you work over four threads instead of two the design will double in size.

Likewise, if the instructions state that the design is worked in cross stitch over two threads of linen and you work over just one thread in either cross stitch or tent stitch, the design size will be halved.

The fabric chosen will also play a large part in determining the size of the design. A design worked over one block of 11-count Aida will be much larger than the same design worked over one thread of linen, 36 threads per inch (25mm)

Using Variegated or Space-Dyed Thread

Variegated or space-dyed thread can give subtle and very beautiful effects if used sympathetically. Consideration must be given to the colour effect where the thread finishes and re-starts. If you have just ended your length at, say, a purple stage, you cannot simply cut and use the next length as it comes from the skein but must select a length that follows the colour sequence. The idea is to merge colours gradually to achieve the desired subtle effect. If working in cross stitch, it is essential to complete each cross individually, instead of working a line of half crosses and then completing the stitches by working back along the line.

Not all space-dyed threads require this treatment. Some are specially dyed with sudden and dramatic changes of colour at very short intervals, giving a totally different look. Whichever type you try, a little practice and experimentation will enable you to produce stunning effects.

CONVERSION CHART

DMC	ANCHOR	DMC	ANCHOR	DMC	ANCHOR	DMC	ANCHOR	DMC	ANCHOR	DMC	ANCHOR	DMC	ANCHOR	DMC	ANCHOR
BLANC	1	372	854	581	28*	738	361	825	162	924	851	992	187*	3685	69
ECRU	387	400	351	597	168*	739	366	826	161*	926	850	993	186*	3687	68
208	111	402	347	598	167*	740	316*	827	9159*	927	848	995	410	3688	66
209	109	407	914*	600	78	741	314	828	158*	928	847	996	433	3689	49
210	108	413	401	601	77	742	303	829	906	930	922	3011	845	3705	35
211	342	414	235	602	63	743	305	830	277*	931	921	3012	843	3706	33
221	897	415	398	603	62	744	301	831	277*	932	343	3013	842	3708	31
223	895*	420	374	604	55	745	300*	832	907*	934	862*	3021	905*	3712	10*
224	893	422	943	605	50	746	386	833	(907)*	935	269*	3022	(899)*	3713	968*
225	892	433	371	606	335	747	928	834	874	936	846	3023	(899)*	3716	25
300	352	434	365	608	333	754	4146*	838	380	937	268*	3024	900*	3721	896*
301	349*	435	901*	610	889	758	868*	839	360*	938	381	3031	360*	3722	895*
304	47	436	363	611	898	760	9*	840	379	939	152	3032	903*	3726	970
307	289	437	362	612	832	761	23	841	378	943	188	3033	830	3727	969*
309	42	444	291	613	853	762	234	842	376	945	881	3041	871	3731	(38)
310	403	445	288	632	936	772	259	844	273*	946	332	3042	870	3733	75*
311	148	451	233	640	393*	775	128	869	944	947	330	3045	888	3740	872
312	979	452	232	642	392	776	24	890	(683)	948	778*	3046	887	3743	869
315	(896)*	453	231	644	396	778	968*	891	29	950	4146*	3047	886	3746	118*
316	969*	469	267*	645	273*	780	310	892	28	951	880	3051	861	3747	120
317	400	470	266*	646	8581*	781	309*	893	27	954	203	3052	859*	3750	(123)
318	399	471	265	647	8581*	782	308	894	26	955	206*	3053	858*	3752	976
319	(217)	472	(278)	648	900*	783	307	895	269*	956	54	3064	883	3753	975
320	215	498	(43)	666	46	791	178	898	359	957	52	3072	274	3755	140
321	9046	500	879	676	891	792	177	899	(40)	958	187*	3078	292	3756	158*
322	978	501	878	677	300*	793	176	900	(326)*	959	186*	3325	129	3760	161*
326	59	502	877	680	901*	794	175	902	72	961	76	3326	36	3761	9159*
327	100	503	876	699	229	796	133	904	258	962	75*	3328	10*	3765	169*
333	119	504	875	700	228	797	132	905	257	963	73	3340	329	3766	167*
334	977	517	170	701	227	798	131	906	256	964	185	3341	328	3768	779
335	(41)	518	(168)*	702	226	799	145	907	255	966	240	3345	268*	3770	276
336	149	519	(167)*	703	239	800	144	909	923	970	324*	3346	267*	3772	914*
340	118*	520	862*	704	283	801	358	910	230*	971	316*	3347	266*	3773	882
341	117	522	860	712	926	806	169*	911	230*	972	298	3348	264	3774	778*
347	13*	523	859*	718	88	807	168*	912	205	973	290	3350	65	3776	349*
349	13*	524	858*	720	326*	809	130	913	204	975	370	3354	74	3777	20
350	(11)	535	(273)*	721	324*	813	160	915	972	976	(309)*	3362	263	3778	9575
351	10*	543	933	722	323	814	45	917	89	977	313	3363	262	3779	868*
352	9*	550	101	725	306	815	22	918	341*	986	246	3364	260	3781	905*
353	6	552	99	726	295	816	(44)	919	340	987	244	3371	382	3782	831
355	341*	553	98	727	293	817	19	920	339	988	243	3607	87	3787	(393)*
356	5975	554	97	729	890	818	48	921	338	989	242	3608	86	3790	903*
367	(216)	561	212	730	924*	819	271	922	337	991	(189)	3609	85	3799	236
368	214	562	210	731	281*	820	134								
369	(213)	563	208	732	281*	822	390								
370	856	564	206*	733	280*	823	150								
371	855	580	924*	734	279	824	164								

*indicates that this Anchor shade has been used more than once

BIBLIOGRAPHY

Backhouse, Janet, *The Illuminated Manuscript*, Phaidon Press, 1979.

Cirker, Blanche (Ed), *Needlework Alphabets and Designs*, Dover, 1975.

Clabburn, Pamela, *The Needleworker's Dictionary*, Macmillan, 1976.

Colby, Averil, *Samplers*, Batsford, 1964.

Crawford, Heather M., *Needlework Samplers of Northern Ireland*, Allingham Publishing, 1989.

Davis, Courtney, *The Celtic Art Source Book*, Blandford Press, 1988.

Deforges, Régine and Dormann, Geneviève, *Alphabets*, Albin Mitchel, 1987.

Huish, Marcus, *Samplers and Tapestry Embroideries*, Dover, 1970.

Leszner, Eva Maria, *Assisi Embroidery*, Batsford, 1988.

Meehan, Aidan, *Celtic Design: A Beginner's Manual*, Thames & Hudson, 1991.

Pesel, Louisa F., *Historical Designs for Embroidery*, Batsford, 1956.

Ring, Betty, *American Needlework Treasures*, E.P. Dutton, 1987.

Sebba, Anne, *Samplers: Five Centuries of a Gentle Craft*, Thames & Hudson, 1979.

Stanwood Bolton, Ethel and Johnson Coe, Eva, *American Samplers*, Dover, 1973.

Stiebner, Erhardt D. and Urban, Dieter, *Initials and Decorative Alphabets*, Blandford Press, 1985.

Swain, Margaret, *Scottish Embroidery*, Batsford, 1986.

Weiss, Rita (Ed), *Victorian Alphabets, Monograms and Names for Needleworkers*, Dover, 1974.

ACKNOWLEDGEMENTS

I would like to thank the following people for their help and support:

First and most of all, my wonderful husband Chris for his help, advice, constructive criticism, love and support; my mother-in-law, Irene, and father-in-law, Jim, for helping to run the business and 'keeping on top of things' at home and therefore contributing much to my sanity; Cathy Cosgrave (with and without leg in plaster) for organising Country Yarns and me; my children, Katie and Nicholas, for understanding that their Mum will shortly return to normal; Jane Greenoff for very helpful advice most unselfishly given.

Di Lewis for her wonderful photography and my warm thanks to all at David & Charles, especially Vivienne Wells for 'steering me through' this project.

My thanks also to the following companies for supplies used in the book:

DMC Creative World, Pullman Road, Wigston, Leicester LE18 2DY, for Zweigart fabric and DMC threads. *Framecraft Miniatures Ltd*, 148/150 High Street, Aston, Birmingham B6 4US, for tree ornaments, brooches and pendants, trinket pots, bookmarks, wooden and brass bell pulls, paperweghts, brass frames, candle-screen and 'jar lacy'. *Craft Creations Ltd*, 1/7, Harpers Yard, Ruskin Road, Tottenham, London N17 8NE, for craft cards (greetings cards with pre-cut mounts). *The Inglestone Collection*, Milton Place, Fairford, Glos GL7 4HR, for linen band and German flower threads. *S & A Frames*, 12 Humber Street, Cleethorpes, Humberside DN35 8NN, for the heart frame, 'church' frame and cross-over frame. *C.M.Offray & Sons Ltd*, Fir Tree Place, Church Road, Ashford, Middlesex TW15 2PH, for ribbons.

The variegated linen thread used in the Welsh Alphabet is from *Brethyn Brith*, Unit 2, Museum of the Welsh Woollen Industry, Drefach-Felindre, Llandysul, Dyfed SA44 5UP. Framing is by *Falcon Art Supplies*, Unit 7, Sedgley Park Trading Estate, George Street, Prestwich, Manchester M25 8WD. Specialist shiny, silk and metallic threads are from *Silken Strands*, 33 Linksway, Gatley, Cheadle, Cheshire SK8 4LA. General needlecraft supplies are from *Hepatica*, 82a Water Lane, Wilmslow, Cheshire SK9 5BB and *Voirrey Embroidery*, Brimstage Hall, Wirral, Cheshire L63 6JA. When writing to any of the above suppliers, please include a stamped addressed envelope for your reply.

INDEX

Numbers in *italic* denote illustrations